From the Crushing To the Crown

I0555071

PRINCESS PAGE ROGERS

www.TrueVinePublishing.org

From the Crushing to the Crown
Princess Page Rogers

Published by True Vine Publishing Co.
810 Dominican Dr. Ste 103
Nashville, TN 37228
www.TrueVinePublishing.org

ISBN- 978-1-956469-59-2 Paperback
ISBN - 978-1-956469-60-8 eBook

First Printing—United States of America

KJV: King James Version
Scripture quotations marked KJV are taken from the Holy Bible King James Version

NIV: New International Version
Scripture quotations taken from The Holy Bible, New International Version® NIV®

ESV: English Standard Version
Scripture quotations marked "ESV" are from the ESV® Bible (The Holy Bible, English Standard Version®), copyright © 2001 by Crossway, a publishing ministry of Good News Publishers. Used by permission. All rights reserved. You may not copy or download more than 500 consecutive verses of the ESV Bible or more than one half of any book of the ESV Bible.

The Message:
Scripture quotations marked MSG are taken from The Message, copyright(c) 1993, 2002,2018 by Eugene H. Peterson. Used by permission of NavPress. All rights reseverd. Represented by Tyndale House Publishers.

Dedication

This book is dedicated to John Eric "Fish" Jones, the best earthly father, friend, and protector ever. Although gone too soon, he will forever be my king. I am the woman I am today because of the man he was to me and for me. I love you always and forever, Daddy. Rest up while your princess continues your legacy.

Table of Contents

Acknowledgements

I am beyond thankful and grateful for all those who encouraged me to tell my story, and even those who did not believe these things should be shared. I would like to thank my boss Golden Hayden. She has listened to my many goals and spent time figuring out how she can be assistance to me to reach goals that had no impact on work. She believed in me and told me I could remain an introvert and still succeed.

I would like to thank my Nashville Girls (Angela, Breanna, Courtney, Kezia, and Sonya) for listening to the many updates and pushing through with me. They have supported me in all things and given honest feedback along the way.

Thank you to my UT Made Forever Friends (Cleasha, Raquel, and Tiara). I could not have come up with the cover design and other important details in this book without your insight. I second-guessed putting all my business out there like this, but you all told me to use my gift. I am allowing God to use me how He sees fit.

Huge thanks to my bestie April Nicole Jackson. She is going to always be real with me no matter what if I want the real or not. In the middle of her running her own business, answering a million of our home-buying questions, she let me know she was proud of me for telling my story. My best friend Selwyn has been ready to buy 100 copies since I first told him about this book. He swears he will need a dictionary to understand it, but I promise it's conversational for almost anyone.

My sweet and gentle Yentel, my sister friend. We have kept each other accountable. We have lifted each other up in prayer and laughed until we fell out from stomach pains. We have had some praise parties and some wine down evenings. Focusing on our goals together and navigating our family dynamics has been an adventure. When I need someone to pray for me, you know I am calling you sister.

Thank you to my amazing family. So many to name. I know I will forget someone. I need to let you all know how much I love you all. I am sure I am looked at as the mean sister, the no nonsense aunt, the drinking cousin, the responsible niece, the accomplished granddaughter, and the nonchalant daughter. I must say, I am literally still trying to figure out life. I may be all these things or none of these things, but I always thought about family above anything else. My hero, my king, Daddy was so big on us staying united. He wanted nothing more than the best for all of us. That is my prayer as well. I will do everything in my power to make it happen for us, God willing.

I had to save the best for last. My husband Calvin Lee Rogers, Jr. I love you more than coffee mornings and ice cream nights. Not many men have the confidence, patience, and understanding you have. Thank you for letting me get on your nerves. I have been told I cater too much to you. I wish I could do more. The way you speak life, your faith in God, your positivity, and your belief in me has gotten me to finally finish this book.

Introduction -
About My Father's Business

When the Lord tells you to act you must act. No matter how uncomfortable you may be. No matter how it is not in your plans. The only plans that matter are those that he has sketched out for us. James 1:22 says be doers of the word, and not hearers only. (ESV) I have fought long and hard with myself and with God on doing what I know He called me to do. I could not keep hearing Him, feeling those convictions, and not move. Even now thinking about it gets me emotional. However, there is only so long I can try to take alternative routes when the path is already laid out for me.

Some would say I was not supposed to be born. My mom reminds me I am the only child of seven (five living) she considered aborting due to the failed relationship with my daddy. Even after she gave birth to me in the late 1980s, I was born a crack baby. Yes, the late Young Dolph was speaking of those like me in his critically acclaimed hit "Preach." Due to the doctors' inability to administer a dosage of crack cocaine to me, they gave me days at most to live. I am 35 years in. So, I know I am here for a reason. While I am thankful my mom had a choice with her body, I am happy she chose me. I am also ecstatic God chose me because at birth I was given a death sentence by the world. I say, I was born to set this world on fire.

Since I was a kid, I pretty much knew what I wanted to do with my life. I knew the job I wanted: to be a lawyer. I was smart. My God given talent was book sense and intelligence. Please do not take this as bragging. I was not artistic, I was not the best dressed kid, I was not the prettiest girl in class, I was not musically inclined, and athletically, other than dance, I was possibly the most challenged in school. Yet, students knew me for my intellect. Occasionally I was that girl who danced. But they knew me as the smart kid, the girl with all A's, or the writer. Romans 12:6 speaks to this specifically. Having gifts that differ according to the grace given to us, let us use them (ESV).... We all cannot be artistic, athletic musicians. God has given us all different gifts and we must use them accordingly.

It all started one year when summer school was an option for childcare my family decided that my big sister and I were going. It was the summer before I started first grade. It was the best thing ever to me. I remember children going out to play or having creativity time that was basically art daily. Well, I did not partake in those many times. Obviously as a kid I wanted to play. But I wanted to write so much more. On the tablet paper we used at that age, with the big lines, I wrote. My teacher was shocked that I had such a great handwriting at my age. Also, I was writing complete sentences. I was not even six yet. That was the beginning of me knowing that writing was a talent the Lord had blessed me with.

Fast forward a few years later. I was writing songs, poems, and short stories in my free time. I had even won a few contests for poetry while in high school. I figured I would keep dancing and writing as hobbies because I had known since third grade how I would make my livelihood. My job was to be an attorney. As a kid, the only thing I enjoyed more than writing was reading. I would read about 12 books in the summer for leisure. Elementary reading was easy and funny. In middle school I was reading books that any middle school girl would read. Things changed when I entered high school. I was reading erotica. My vocabulary expanded and my mind expanded even more. My mind was fixated on this erotica. It was so consuming. It was even in my dreams. By the time I got to college I was reading about four novels a summer: all erotica. During that time, I decided I would write a novel. I would write a Black erotica novel. By this time, I had writer's high, so I started the process. I gave myself deadlines. It never came to pass.

While in law school I realized the importance of writing. Persuasive writing, informative writing, and analytical writing were all important. I set out to become the best writer I could be. I could do briefs and memorandums in hours, while it would take days for others to finish. I was thinking yes, my writing skills are finally going to pay off for me. Well, I still wanted to write a novel. Legal writing is the exact opposite of writing a novel. That did not change my mind. In college I had started my erotica novel, but I had absolutely no time to work on it while in law school. (Those were the hardest three years in academia I ever encountered.)

After law school and after the bar (twice), I decided I would start back on my novel. I tried. I really did put time and effort into writing this thing. There was absolutely nothing I could put on the page. I would read over what I had written and change it up in order to follow that out. It did not work. Life had happened and I felt my broken heart stopped me from writing. I no longer wrote poems or songs and for the life of me this novel was going nowhere fast.

I was still writing legal essays. I had begun writing some of my prayers in a journal. After I recommitted my life to Christ again (yes recommitted again) the Holy Spirit told me I was never supposed to write an erotica anything. He told me I will write, but it will be for the glory of God. The Lord will not give you a gift that will be glorifying the world of sin. If it is truly from Him, know that your gift should be used for good. Yes, you have free will. In the end, you have to answer to Him and only Him. I learned then my assignment was to write for His glory. I would tell whomever willing to read of my

11

God's goodness. Not my granddad's God, not my mom's God, but my God I had grown in relationship with for myself.

At the time the Holy Spirit told me I would write for His glory I started going back and forth with Him. Let me just say, I was excited to write for God. I was ready to do what He wanted me to do. I asked Him every night to use me. But I had to make sure this was not something I was led to do while saying it was the Holy Spirit that led me. I needed signs to know exactly what He called me to do. I did not want to be outside of His will. I said I will blog. I can do that. The Lord said no. I said but my sisters in Christ are blogging, and I want to blog. He said Princess no. I pouted. That is typical from any Daddy's girl. I asked, "Well Lord, what is it that You want me to do?" He continuously placed "testify" in my spirit. I was not having it. I knew that could not be what God had for me. My then friends who knew some of my story had said since college, "Princess you should really tell your story. People would really be blessed by it." A quick "no thanks" was always my response. I do not want people in my business. I continued to get confirmation from people around me, those the Lord had sent as laborers. Pastors' sermons and other communication to me were all about sharing my story. I brushed that under the rug. My pastor made references to it many times. I ignored him saying every time that this particular message was not for me. I knew deep down it really was for me.

The Lord said you want me to use you I am telling you what to do and you are running. I said well are You sure? What about publishers? What about my personal life that I just do not want people to know? I'm not sure if God was laughing at me or shaking His head at me. But of course, He was sure! I said well I need another sign.

I was driving down the street in tears after praising Him on the way home from work, and He dropped that He wanted me to share my testimony in my spirit yet again. I said okay, God. If this is what you want, I know my mom would know. She is a professing follower of Christ. Right then the Holy Spirit told me not to call her; it is not her decision. I had already dialed her number. I am used to her not answering; I would leave a voicemail, but this time the call was not going through at all. I was unable to reach my mom that day. The next day I talked to my mom, and I told her how the day before God did not want me to talk to her about something. She said well tell me now sweetie. I told her and she was totally against it. She said you do not need to tell people your business. If you tell people how much money you make you will become a target. She gave me stories of people in church testifying then getting robbed. All I was thinking was mom I do not make enough money for anyone to rob me unless they want to practice, plus that is not what He wants me to testify about.

As I walked into bible study that night the Lord said, "This is why you did not need to consult her or anyone else. I know what I have told you to do." And at that moment I knew why He did not want me to talk to my mom or anyone about it. That was my final sign. After going back and forward with Him about it an extremely long time I realized this was the calling He had on my life. I laughed out loud and said okay God we are on one accord. I was rejoicing for this revelation. He did not give me the gift of writing to turn people to sexual sin which is likely what would happen if I were writing erotica. He gave me this gift to glorify Him. I decided to fully submit, although it was actually already decided for me. This is me submitting. I pray that someone reads my story or hears about my story, and it can help them turn to God, draw closer to God, love Him more, or even go after their own God given assignment. Do not pass go, do not collect $200. Run straight to Him.

Ch. 1
Meeting Me

Sunday, January 26, 2020, Kobe Bryant died. I got calls and texts as I drove from church. I was in complete disbelief. I told my husband Calvin not only could I not drive any longer, but I also no longer felt like grocery shopping, and it was probably best we grabbed something at a restaurant. As I sat there waiting to think about what to order since my appetite temporarily left me, all I could think about was who Kobe was to so many people. I was blessed to see him play. I even met him after a surprise birthday dinner for a friend in Memphis. But I did not know him. Yet, his death had such an impact on me and so many others. We were fans of more than the game. We were fans of who we believed him to be. A great leader, a competitor like no other, a family man, a businessman, someone who never settled for average, a human who had made mistakes and learned from them and allowed them to make him want better. I started to think about who I was. I have never wanted to be a huge celebrity with no privacy. Yet, you can impact the people around every day by being who you are. So, who was I? Was I sure of myself? Was I a true Christian? Did I love myself? Did I love my neighbors? How was I making anyone want to be better than they were before? Did I even know myself?

Let us just dive right in. While I did not know it then, I had a problem with being alone when I was younger. This chapter will touch on the dysfunction that I called relationships. I know I am more than a relationship, but at some point in my life, I thought that was the most important thing. Weird, but it'll all make sense by the end of this chapter. Since I can remember, there were always people around me. I am the second of five children. I grew up with a good amount of people in my house. For the most part, I enjoyed my large family. They stayed out of my way and vice versa. Yet I love my four siblings unconditionally. When I moved from my mom's home, I began to find other things to keep my attention. There was no longer a huge, young, and active family. As a middle school girl, boys kept my attention.

Against my family wishes, I had a boyfriend since I was in eighth grade. My first boyfriend Dewayne was the coolest and cutest guy in my middle school. Or it may have just been that way in my eyes. He was part of the cool crew of guys. And being part of the cool crew of girls, of course I had to talk to him. Our relationship made a lot of the other girls envious of me. Dewayne loved all the glory of girls fighting over him. But I liked him. I told myself I was not fighting over a boy I was fighting in self-defense of girls who came at me. I almost believed that I was fighting for self-defense. I totally looked over the fact that Dewayne was getting praise for the fight.

After this fight, a Black eye, and a school suspicious, I still did not break up with him. At some point, Dewayne had been kicked out of school for something crazy, I am sure. When another guy showed interest in me, I was also interested. Let's call him Aiden. He was one of the stars of our basketball team, so I did not waste time talking to him.

I went to every game, home and away, cheering for Aiden. We lost more games than we won, but I was there by his side. I was going to stick beside him. After basketball season, I heard rumors of Aiden and some girl Trina going out. Of course, she and I eventually had a conversation about it. Trina told me it was true. When I confronted Aiden, he said because I was not putting out, "it" kind of just happened. Trina was not the only one. I chose to ignore the other girls at the games yelling for him too. But because this girl came to me, I sort of respected her more than the others. Aiden and I stopped talking, and I ran back to Dewayne. I had now, at 13 years old, found validation in a man.

Why did I run back to my ex-boyfriend Dewayne? Because, in my eyes, I did not need to be single. I needed to have a boyfriend who was into me and would give me all his free time. I was beyond stupid for him. I was still an honor student; therefore, I was not monitored a lot. There was a lot I could do. I knew that having a boyfriend meant I was not alone. I was always envied by others who wanted what I had. Long story short, I was headed for self -destruction. Any boyfriend I had at the time became my total focus.

It was baseball season. This extremely cute guy Kendrick played baseball. Tall, chocolate, broad shoulders, huge white smile. He was a lot smarter than the other two guys I called my boyfriend, so I figured I was making better life decisions for myself. I became the assistant to the baseball team so I could travel with the team. I felt I had to support my new boo, Kendrick. I kept score. I cheered him on. I washed uniforms. We talked after games. We hugged. This guy was a good kid which was boring. We broke up like most young relationships based on all the wrong things. I continued talking to Dewayne although he was still kicked out of school.

The summer before high school, I remember feeling like something was missing. I would turn to poetry to hash out all my feelings. I felt better after getting it all on paper, but that void was not filled. I prayed to God asking Him to help me. But I was not asking Him to fill me with The Holy Ghost. I was not asking for comfort. I wanted the emptiness I felt to go away. That was my prayer. At an incredibly young age I learned codependency. I felt that another human could validate me, make me feel better about whom I was, keep me happy, and block out any voids I had. The Lord says, "You shall have no other gods before me." (Exodus 20:3 NKJV). I did not think I was putting anyone before God. I prayed. I loved God. But I was unintentionally putting a relationship with a significant other before God. I depended on my boyfriend to make me feel better. It was the start of a horrible pattern that went on for years.

High school was totally different. Everyone looked so...grown. I mean, where did these adult children come from? I was a little nervous. I just did what came naturally to me. I enrolled in honors courses. I always had a lot of homework. I complained, but it was not actually hard. Guys in my classes had not seen me in middle school because this was a different part of town. Many upperclassmen were very intrigued by me and started showing interest almost immediately. I did not like the attention because people assumed I was sexually active already. I started high school at 13 years old since by birthday was just a month after classes started, but I developed early. Hips, butt, breasts were already upon me. But I was a child and as soon as I opened my mouth it was evident. I knew what guys were thinking, and I was so not interested in going there with anyone. After all, I was still recovering from a breakup.

Long story short, I ended up in a class with all upperclassmen. The guys laid out the red carpet every day for me, but it was one guy who did not really seem to like me. Let's call him Jay. Jay defended me against all the other guys. We became friends.

I found out he was in eleventh grade. He was not a smart guy, but he was funny. I was not attracted to Jay at all. He was not short, but he was not tall either. He had a little tummy I guess what today we would call a dad bod, but he was in high school. There was not much striking about his extremely dark complexion that I usually love. While Jay stood up for me when the hounds came out ready to prey, I did his homework and said nice things to him occasionally. We exchanged phone numbers and before I knew it, I had another boyfriend just like that. Jay said hanging with me was like hanging with the guys. It could have been because I was still not able to have a real boyfriend yet. He gained a lot of popularity at school while dating me. However, it was the exact opposite when it came to family life. My mom found out her sweet, innocent, intelligent daughter was entertaining a much older boy. She was livid. She tried to call the cops on us. She attempted to pray those demons out of me. I was scared for Jay, yet my mom thought I was demonic. I felt she merely did not understand. Her not approving made me like him even more.

Jay had started seeing one of the most sought-after girls in ninth grade: me. Although by the spring semester I was old news and no longer the new hot commodity, he continued to gain popularity. This came with problems for me. Other women began approaching him. In one instance, a young lady addressed Jay, and it started a fight against her with me and my cousins. This was now my second fight because of a boy. He too loved the attention and glory. I explained to Jay I was not for the cheating and whatever was said was too intense for me. I was sure he learned his lesson.

At some point I decided I was ready to take my relationship with Jay to the next level. I knew it was not of God. My mom told me plenty of times as a Christian I was supposed to wait until I was married to have sex. While I knew she was right, I cannot exactly say why I wanted to do it. It could have been me wanted to be rebellious since I had this "goody two shoes" image, or it could have been me just wanting to be in control. I was not living under my mom's roof, so I did not understand how she was able to make the day-to-day decisions in my life while I lived with my grandma.

I told Jay I was ready. He was shocked but excited. He planned a spot for us to go. Because I could not date, my big sister and cousin went with me to Jay's cousin's house. And just like that, it happened.

After a couple weeks of getting over that pain, I decided I wanted to try at it again. I told Jay it was time, and he obliged. This time we went to another one of his cousin's houses. Because I had a female friend pick me up, I did not have to have my sister and cousin in tow. I was at ease not having my family supervising me. Well done, Princess. I was keeping this boyfriend forever.

I remember feeling like I was in complete control. I was so deep in lust I truly felt I had made the right decision. I felt full. I felt complete. I was so happy. This man consumed my thoughts all day and all night. He was my godsend. No one really waited to marriage anymore anyway. My mom was totally old fashioned. In the back of my head, I knew I did not want kids with Jay I could not even see myself marrying him. But I wanted him and only him at that time anyway.

As time passed, Jay continuously told me that I should join his church to ensure that I would make it to heaven. The denomination of the church he attended believes that their denomination is the only church that will enter heaven. Converting is the only way he would marry me. Well, I never considered converting. I knew it was more than one church entering heaven. I also did not feel confident that I wanted him to be my husband. I always desired more. Jay was cool, but he was not it.

We always had faith-based conversations. Jay knew the bible very well. I did not let it intrigue me too much because I knew the devil also knew the bible. Still, I felt better knowing he was knowledgeable. He knew God just as I knew God. We both grew up in the church. We made sure that we did not go too far from Him. Although sin separated us from God, we knew He would forgive us, and that He loved us unconditionally. This man loved me, and he knew God. He was obviously good for me. Surely this little sexual immorality would not keep us from Christ. Yes, I was really that lost in sin.

Somehow, I lacked knowledge at fourteen years old that my seventeen-year-old boyfriend might not be the best for me. Jay's senior year in high school (my sophomore year), our relationship continued. This instantly brings a scripture to mind. All other sins a person commits are outside the body but whoever sins sexually sins against their own body. (1 Corinthians 6:18 NIV). Thinking that sexual sin was nothing was the wrong take. Yet, as a kid I did not think twice about my decision.

But things changed with me and Jay. He began verbally and physically abusing me. It would be mostly when it was only the two of us or when we were around his friends. All those who knew told me I deserved better. For the most part, everyone else was in the dark. I never had bruises or noticeable marks. I felt like the good outweighed the bad and I was not alone.

When he graduated and I started eleventh grade, I realized all my friends were his friends, and they were all gone. Jay would pick me up after school, give me weekly allowance, and buy me food. I felt the abuse was minor to all the nice things he did. My grandma insisted that we all get jobs at sixteen. When that time came for me to work, Jay was still providing for me, so I did not have to work. One may wonder if my family knew or if I concealed this from them. My grandma was very much aware of how I was financing my life at the time. She encouraged this since I was not working. She could not afford to get all my necessities. My grades never slipped. I was old enough to date freely now. We still had some good times in the relationship although they were few and far in between now. Oh yes, Jay was now cheating with women his age that were no longer in school. Deep down I knew it was time to let it go. But I could not give up all the benefits that came with this relationship. I had already become too dependent on him. That was problematic, but at the time I was thinking Jay was supposed to be my life.

While I was allowing Jay to be my "everything" I was unknowingly making man my idol again. God is a jealous God. Remember Exodus 20:3? The Lord never wanted me, or anyone else, to put anyone before Him. He wanted to be who I looked to when times were rough, when I needed a friend, and when I was making major life decisions. Making a man my "everything" was me idolizing man. I thought highly enough of those little boyfriends that I would take the bumps and bruises. I wanted them in my life. In every relationship I demanded more and more out of the man. I felt these things meant he really liked me, he loved me, he wanted me over other girls, I was valued, I was important. I felt that having someone to love me defined me. I was searching for myself in a relationship with a man. I was still blind to who I really was in Christ.

For where your treasure is, there your heart will be also. (Matthew 6:21 NIV). This verse makes me think about a pirate with a chest full of diamonds and gold. I imagine him loving those things in the chest more than anything. I see him so consumed by what was in the chest he lets it take over. This is basically how I had become with whatever boyfriend I had at the time. That boyfriend was my treasure. My heart was with that man. Yes, I still gave God some time here and there. I still let Him know I recognized His presence, but I was not treasuring Him. I treasured the relationship with my little boyfriends. I was all in heart and soul. It was so sad and pathetic. I can say that about myself now because I recognize how empty that Princess was during that time.

It takes knowing you are empty to start wanting to be full. Relationships with these guys never seemed to fill me up. I would want it badly. After a huge fight over something small I would break it off. Or I would act a fool on my boyfriend getting on his last nerve and he would call it quits. Then once I was lonely again, not wanting to face me, I instantly prayed. Lord, please give me this person back. If You get us back together, I promise I would never let it go again. I will be the best girlfriend. I will make sure I stay with him and do right by him. Please God. And sooner than later my boyfriend and I get back together. We are nice and all in love until something else hits the fan. The unhealthy and unholy cycle continued. Every relationship was toxic. It was not solely the man. I had quite a few toxic traits myself. Yet, I felt there were normal because it was not like I had the best examples around me. From a mom who married because he accepted her two children although she was still in love with my dad to a grandma who divorced my cheating granddad only to remarry and continue to be cheated on and abused, but since the bills were paid, all was well.

I was tired. I was sick and tired. It was like a game to me. I was fighting for attention, fighting to be loved, fighting to get my way, fighting to have this person in my life. I did all of this because I did not want to feel alone. The entire time the Lord was with me. Do not be afraid or terrified, for the Lord your God goes with you; He will never leave you nor forsake you. (Deuteronomy 31: 6 NIV). That is just so powerful. All the time I am literally fighting to keep my boyfriends in my life in order for me not to feel alone, the Lord my God was with me the entire time.

In the past when I felt lonely, I clung to a man. Now I know when I get that feeling, I need to cling to God. He completely fills me up with Him. I get so full, so at peace, so joyful I cannot help but praise Him. The lonely feeling goes away. Jesus says He will pray to the Father, and He will give us another Helper or Advocate. (John 14:16 NKJV, NIV). This Helper or Advocate is the Holy Spirit. Because the Holy Spirit is with me comforting me, I do not feel alone. But I had to seek Him. I had to be intentional about seeking Him. I did not find God sitting in my room texting crazy stuff to guys. I had to block, delete, unfriend, and unfollow all those distractions. I sought Him on my face praying. I am not saying go get on your face while at work, in class, at your sister's friend's cousin's birthday party. What I am saying is get some alone time with God. Just the two of you, call out to Him. Talk to Him. Cry to Him if need be. Standing, sitting, kneeling, facedown, or however you decide to pray is not important. What is important is that you are isolating yourself from the rest of the world and being completely focused on God. He hears these prayers according to Psalm 66:19. In John 10:27 Jesus says He knows your voice.

Strangely enough, I found myself in these deep prayers and conversations with God. I asked Him to reveal things about me that I did not know. I asked Him to help me work on the things I did know about me that were unpleasing. I found out I tell more little white lies than most. Why? Because I want to make people feel better about themselves. I can find ways to lift people's spirits without lying. And people deserve honesty; I should be that person if it can be done in a Christ-like manner. A false witness will not go unpunished, and a liar will be destroyed. (Proverbs 19:9 NLT). Even little white lies are lies. I am trying to inherent the kingdom of God not the emotions of man. I had to seriously reevaluate some things. I also found out I was a manipulator. I would use my intellect, my persuasive speech, or whatever else to get what I wanted without verbalizing this is what I want. I always felt I was giving them an offer they could not refuse. Once my dear friend and sister in Christ Alyssa revealed to me that a manipulative spirit was also part of the Jezebel spirit, I knew the Lord had to deliver me from that. I instantly went into prayer about that thing. I was tested, and because of Him I have been successfully passing thus far.

Even Jesus warned against jezebel in Revelations 2:18-29. I knew it was something I had to rid myself of and God was my only help.

Some things I am still working on, and I am constantly finding out different things about me. But it feels good to know me now. I can go to lunch or dinner solo and not feel lonely or even self-conscious. I quickly let anyone with questions know I am on a date with Bae: Jesus is Bae. It is a process, but the process is beautiful. No matter where you are, if you do not feel like you know yourself do something about it. It took me years and I know it was worth it. Ask the Lord to reveal to you your true self. Watch in amazement as He does just that. This gives you the opportunity to be a better Christian and a better person for your "right now" and your "not yet." Meeting me has been a shocker yet amazingly refreshing. No matter where you are in life, it's never too late to finally meet you. Once you know who you are, you know what you like and do not like. Then you have the opportunity to work on yourself. Work on having the spirit of excellence while still exuding joy and peace. Whatever area you see needs work, do it. Also water the good things about yourself. Do not let the death of someone you admire make you wonder who you are. But if that is what it takes, do the work anyway.

There will be some things you do not like when you truly see yourself. The only way to rid these bad traits is to recognize them. It took being damaged by relationship after relationship, I am referring to family, friends, and all the above, for me to see I needed to find myself. Your process may be similar or different. Either way, trust God through it all, and enjoy the journey.

Ch 2
From Control Issues to Playing in the Background

When it comes to life decisions it is tough to relinquish control. You can get in your own way if you are not careful. A great woman once said, "Make sure you are not the weapon formed against yourself that is causing you not to prosper." That woman is Janet Jackson. I am not sure if she said it, but she posted it on her Instagram, and I absolutely love her, so I am sticking with those are her words. There are times when you think you have it all under control. You are 'making moves' and everything seems to be going well. But it is not you; it is His grace. There was a time I can remember having a text conversation with one of my longtime friends William. He told me how proud of me he was. William felt I was doing well for myself. I was telling him how I am not good at making my own decisions, but William said from his vantage point he sees that I have made great decisions in my life.

For the record, every decision that I made on my own was based off emotions and with someone else in mind. I usually made these decisions on highs. During my last year of law school, I was dating someone who had recently retired from the military, Jersey. He lived outside of Chicago. He was in the process of buying a home. I would make the four-hour drive down from Lansing, Michigan to do viewings with Jersey to show my support. He made it clear that he wanted me to take the Illinois bar exam and to live with him. I was unsure if I wanted to in case things did not work out with us; I did not want to end up homeless. I remember having a conversation with an ex, Eli about me possibly moving to Chicago. I was still head over heels with Eli, but because we were trying the friend thing, I wanted to know his thoughts. Eli told me he did not think me moving to Chicago after law school was a good idea. He felt it was best for me to come back home and take the Tennessee bar first. If I wanted to take another bar later, then I would always have the option to decide where I wanted to practice. My heart dropped. The biggest smile came over my face. I am sure Eli could feel my smile in every word I said. I knew that him wanting me back in Tennessee instead of Illinois was because Eli wanted me closer to him. We had been twelve hours away for three years. Surely, he wanted to rekindle things. I thanked Eli for being so helpful in my decision making. I told Jersey I decided on taking the Tennessee bar first and of course the Illinois bar would be right after. I also explained how I wanted more before I moved in with him. He seemed to understand and was not ready to propose. Jersey never questioned my reason for not wanting to move to Chicago yet, and I'm sure it made sense to be licensed in my home state.

A few weeks later I talked to Eli about him wanting me to be closer to him. I was super excited thinking he was going to profess his love to me yet again. That was a negative. His jarring response said it all. Because Eli was a very logical thinker, he felt it only made sense to prepare for home first because it was home. It had nothing to do with us, nothing to do with him wanting me. He simply thought it was sensible. I was crushed for assuming. Eli asked me, as nicely as he could although I knew he was fed up, to stop making decisions with him in mind. He knew I had done it for years, since high school in fact, and he wanted me to choose me because he was choosing him, and that part was obvious.

So, texting my friend William about what he thought was my great decisions, I could not take the credit. I had to explain to him that it was not me it was God leading me that led to good positions. All the things that had gone well in my life were not from my decisions they were from me allowing the Lord to have control. I put the decision in His hands because I had no idea how I should handle things. William had a hard time grasping what I was saying to him. I tried to explain in depth. I remember when I followed what I wanted to do I always came back with a bad report. I would have to get my way. I would finesse the situation to get what I wanted right then. But those decisions were not of God. They were self-gratifying. I even knew I was not doing things the way the Lord would have wanted me to do them. But I would enhance the volume of everything around me to drown out His voice. If I could not hear God, I would not feel as guilty for the decisions I made.

As I child I remember my mother telling me I must do things God's way. Whenever I went outside of His will something bad would happen. I was thinking maybe my mother is telling me this to get me to do what she wanted me to do. I was not about to succumb to her way. Even as a little girl I had a hard time believing that doing something my way could be harmful to me in the long run. When my mother revealed to us that we had to do things God's way I remember pondering on it that night. I was a little fearful, but I was usually up for any challenge. I woke up the next day with my mind made up: I was going to be in control. I had become accustomed to thanking God for waking me up every morning. That morning I told Him, "Okay God I am going to do things my way, I am in control." I was nervous but I was also smiling. Now that I think about it, it was very creepy. I felt uncovered the entire day. I do not remember the ends and outs of that day, but I do remember getting in trouble at school normally. It resulted in me getting in trouble at home. I never got in trouble. I was a teacher's pet. I was the walk the straight-line kid around adults out of respect. I also never wanted a bad reputation. I had another talk with God that evening. This time I said tearfully, "Okay God. I will do what You want and how You want me to do it. Doing this my way is not worth it. I do not want to be in control anymore."

Even then I could grasp that my life is not my own. Jesus said, "With man this is impossible, but with God all things are possible." (Matthew 19:26 NIV). I had to allow Him to control this life He had given to me. Yes, I was going to be a kid and do things kids would do, but under no circumstances was I to intentionally defy the Father. That is what I had done in hopes of proving my mom wrong. I wish that were all it took for me to realize I did not have control over my life. I wish that encounter had stuck with me all the days of my life and forced me to completely give God free reign over my life that He so graciously gave to me. Like almost every lesson you learn in life, it takes multiple times before you get it right.

On one occasion as an adult, I wanted to talk to this particular guy Spooner. I had never talked to a bad boy. He was from the old neighborhood, and he found me on social media. I was thinking okay he likes me. I had a huge crush on Spooner when I was a teen, and I felt this was now the perfect opportunity to pursue that. He was no one I would seriously consider marrying, but at the time I felt it would be fun. I felt he was right for me at this time in my life for a few reasons. We exchanged numbers and would talk for hours. When I could not talk, we would text for hours. I told Spooner the issues I was having with my relationship (or lack thereof) with Eli at the time. He wanted to give me the attention I was missing so he would fly to see me monthly. I felt it was genuinely nice of him. Spooner also bought me whatever he felt I needed and most of the things I wanted. I knew he was not a godly guy, but he was fun for the time being and he was cool. I mean, who knows, he could find God while he was kicking it with me. Although that was not really on my mind. I wanted to be in control of who I gave my time to. Also, part of me wanted to show him I was not someone out to get him like everyone else in his life. At the time, the person I deeply wanted to give my time to was Eli, but he was not able to deliver. It seems like Spooner cared enough and wanted to have fun as well. He had financed my life, helped build my confidence, and given more attention than I could have asked. Whether or not I was doing what was right, I was doing what I wanted to do. Outside of Spooner my life was hectic, but I felt like I was in complete control of that friendship.

Correction, it ended horribly just a year later. There is no other way to explain it. I will spare you the details. We did not see eye to eye and had to part ways. When we parted ways, it appeared that I had lost complete control of my life in that short time span. I was worst off from when I started. My bills were not getting paid, I did not have gas in my car, I could not even turn to my family for help. Correction, I refused to turn to my family for help. I was not at a point where I was willing to do so just yet. I was hysterical. I did not even know what to do with my time. I should have been studying since I was in my second year of law school, but I was so distraught.

After fighting it, I turned down the world. I refused to get on social media, answer calls or texts that were not important and hanging out was completely out of the question. I allowed myself to hear God's voice. He was there ready to take back the control that was rightfully His. He did not make me feel bad for trying to do things my own way. He wanted to heal every wound I had received. I was thinking to myself wondering why I did not allow Him to move in my life sooner. But I realized it was a host of things. It was me trying to get the glory. It was me being afraid to let go knowing the result would be unfavorable to me. It was me not wanting to feel like I failed. It was all about me not wanting to be shamed or embarrassed. I had free will and I chose to do with it what I desired.

When going through times when you may want to keep control of your relationship, your job, your finances, your family, remember His Word. Proverbs states many are the plans in the mind of a man, but it is the purpose of the Lord that will stand. (Proverbs 19:21 ESV). No matter how you think you will get the job done perfectly; make sure you consult your Heavenly Father first. Decisions made without His approval first could be detrimental to your livelihood. You may feel it is time to move away, this job has room for growth although your heart and passion is somewhere else, you have put too much energy into this relationship to let go at this point. Take it all to God first. God will not tell your business to family and friends or have your life's most intricate details plastered on social media. The best thing about going to God is that you do not have to be overwhelmed with making decisions alone. You have God to make that decision for you. There is so much peace in knowing He will handle all your problems. The Lord will fight for you; you need only to be still. (Exodus 14:14 NIV).

While some matters are easy to give to God, others can be tough. The small task of picking the route to take daily is no longer in my control. If the interstate is my usual and the Lord wants me to take a residential route that could be longer, I know to follow Him. However, when making decisions that could impact you long-term, in the back of your mind you may still think you know what is best for you. Or you may not want to do what is best for your future; you want instant gratification. Give it to God anyway. Allow Him to move. The Bible says some things will not happen easily, you will have to pray and fast to get the answer from God. (Matthew 17:21 NKJV). The disciples could not get a demon out of the boy. When Jesus said come out the demon came out, and the boy was cured. Jesus explained to the disciples in private it takes more than just faith to cast out some demons. When a major decision is before you and you are having a hard time relinquishing control, turn to prayer and fasting. God will reveal to you what He would have you do. I happily gave it all to God, but only after I was tired of learning the hard way.

While driving home one day I heard a song by one of my favorite gospel rappers. I felt that someone else knew exactly how I was feeling. I was getting in my own way. Trial after trial and failed test after failed test I eventually learned how to play the background. When I started playing the background and allowed the Lord to take the lead, my life felt worth living. Once I was satisfied playing a supporting role and letting the leading role of my life go to My Heavenly Father all was well. The same can happen for you. Invoke His will. You must want to allow God to lead your life. He will not force Himself in the driver's seat. He will be that backseat driver until you finally decide driving is not for you. When your will lines up with the plan He has for your life, God will show you that nothing is impossible. But if you want to be in control of your life, He will let you do so. You must care enough about yourself and about your life to give Him the keys, the leading role, the control, for everything. Trust Jesus with all things. Trust in the Lord with all your heart and lean not on your own understanding; in all your ways submit to Him, and He will make your paths straight. (Proverbs 3:5-6 NIV). If you truly trust God with all your heart, you will give Him total control of everything. Relinquish control and enjoy His sovereign hand driving. The view is nice from the backseat when your chauffeur is Christ.

Ch 3
Trust in Him or Naw?

To put it lightly, my trust is almost nonexistent. I have been let down more times than I want to remember. The one person I felt I could always turn to because he would never lie to me, and he would always be there, hurt me in ways unimaginable. I vowed to never trust again. I vowed to keep a hardened heart. I refused to trust another person. I know this may sound a little extreme. It is important to get to the root of trust issues. It does not usually begin where it seems to begin. It is usually something from the past that has been suppressed or forgotten that caused the current failure to trust others. For me, it started with my parents.

I know how it feels to be that fatherless child growing up. Yes, we had a stepfather in the home, and we loved him very much. But he was not my dad, and we knew that from day one. He did not act like a dad. He was more like an assistant to my mother. He was nice enough for the most part, but I was never confused about who my father was. My first memory of my daddy was a visit to the penitentiary. I think I was about 3 or 4 years old at the time. He was tall like a giant. His skin was the kind of beautiful dark like being in the sun all summer long and was still smooth and youthful. He had the biggest smile, but a voice that sounded like a roar. I remember thinking wow his voice is like the voice of God. He was strong and could pick me and my older sister up at the same time. For the most part, this is how I got to know my daddy. All my childhood memories were consumed with prison visits in addition to endless phone calls and later letters once I could write back.

My father came home from completing an eleven-year sentence on drug charges when I was in middle school only to do the "in and out" thing until after I graduated from college. He continued to write and tell me how much he loved me. Yes, I believed he loved me. But I did not understand how he expected me to believe him when he always said he was coming home for me when he continued to leave me. My trust was broken. At the age of sixteen I made the decision never to go to prison to see him again. I told him if he really loved me, he would stop doing things that would keep him away from me. I did not want the money or any of the things he could provide financially; I wanted his time. I never stopped loving him, but I knew I could not depend on him to be the present father I read about or saw on television. I could not invite him to a daddy daughter dance. I could not ask him to chaperone a field trip. I did not expect my daddy to tuck me in at night after we had an eventful day at the park eating ice cream. As the years went by without him, my trust grew weaker and weaker. No one stood a chance.

My mother was not much better. I also know deep down she loves me very much. However, she was in and out of my life since adolescence. She had a constant struggle with staying clean from a longtime drug addiction. She would be good for months, but it never lasted too long. I was not aware what trust was at the time, but I knew I did not believe her or in her. As a young child, I was obsessed with her and wanted to be everywhere she was. She was curvy, wide hips with a small bust. Paper bag brown with huge dimples. Her smile was like the sunshine. Now that I think about it, that could have been her gold tooth that was like sunshine, but who knows at this point. When she was not around, I made up grand scenarios in my head as to how happy and full of joy she would be when she finally came home. Of course, when we did see her after one of her many binges, it was the opposite. She would be happy to see us yes, but there was an emptiness in her eyes I will never forget. I knew she was shame for her actions. To be honest, I was not mad at her. It was hard to believe she would ever get clean, finally rid that demon, and be a loving mother I longed for daily. I never buried the dreams of having a functional relationship, but I also did not expect it. My trust went out the window with my mother at an incredibly young age. I was numb to her antics and much of the antics around me.

I never gave up on either of them. I continued to have hope that my parents would finally get it together. Even when I knew I could not get the relationship I wanted as a teen, I still wanted them to at least know me. With my dad, we grew close again once I went to college. He came home after I graduated undergrad and had been my biggest supporter and an amazing father. I shared just about everything with him even when he did not want to hear about boy problems. I would call him all times of the night just to ask what he thought about something so random. I loved the access I had to him. We cheered on our Cowboys together, the Grizzlies together, and talked constantly just checking on each other. He was finally mine. However, the bliss was short lived when my father was murdered my last year in my 20s. And the fairy tale of a loving mother quickly turned back to reality time after time. When you are the only willing party to make amends, you become mentally and emotionally drained.

When you have lost trust in your parents it is extremely hard to find trust in other places. It is also dangerous because you unknowingly seek trust from other places. Whenever someone came into my life, I questioned their motives and if it would ever be something real. Because of my lack of trust, I am sure I pushed many people away some good people. Unfortunately, I was not at a place where I could trust anyone. Things were real bleak with my parents, and Eli felt the wrath of every insecurity and trust issue as a result. Like many, he became a mere casualty due to my lack of trust from years' past. I felt no one was truly there for me. Yes, I had loved ones who helped, and I know they loved me as well. I will never pretend I could not pick up the phone and ask for help. I had lived with my uncle, my grandma, and my aunt. I am blessed to have other family members who could step it. It did not change how I felt, and no one could ever replace a parent.

I gained this "Me, Myself, and I" mentality. Part of it may have come from the R&B music I was listening to at the time. Beyonce sang about being alone. Many artists expressed loneliness, feelings of being incomplete, and sadness. Unfortunately, to me that was the life I was living. I felt I was the only person I had. Everyone else had fallen short. Everyone else was not trustworthy. But when I started my serious walk with Christ, I was convicted on that "Me, Myself, and I" thought process. Jesus said, "surely I am with you always, even to the end of the age." (Matthew 28:20 NIV). He was and is with me. He is with all of us.

I refused to have this "woe is me" attitude. I knew my story was for His glory. His word says He will be a father to the fatherless. (Psalm 68:5). I turned to God to be my parents, my friend, and my husband. (John 15:15; Isaiah 54:5). When He became my everything, finally my life changed. I always smiled to mask my true feelings, but finally I smiled and meant it. The Lord was doing a new thing in me, and it felt amazing. (Isaiah 43:19).

I instantly felt horrible that I even could think He was not with me. That was a misplaced feeling from the enemy as well. Many people have felt they had no one to trust, no one to turn to with issues. Let us take Jesus for example. Even on the cross He asked God why He had forsaken Him. (Matthew 27:46). He knew what He had to do for man, but in His humanity the burden was a bit much. God was with Jesus, and God is with us. The Lord has always been with me. Nothing could separate us from the love of God. Paul said I am convinced that neither death nor life, neither angels nor demons, neither the present nor the future, nor any powers, neither height nor depth, nor anything else in all creation, will be able to separate us from the love of God that is in Christ Jesus our Lord. (Romans 8: 38-39 NIV). If you cannot trust anyone you can trust God. And He is the best because at least you know He will not tell your business to anyone else.

The bible is a beautiful book in that the answer to everything is strategically placed. It says trust in the Lord with all your heart and lean not on your own understanding (Proverbs 3:5 NKJV). I was putting my trust in all the wrong places. If you are trying to fill voids, turn to God. If you feel no one is in your corner, turn to God. If you have lost trust, turn to God. Everyone else will fail you. And it is not you. It is because you have such high expectations for them. You believe someone or something can make whatever wrong better. Temporarily, that may work. But as soon as you put your hope and faith in man, he will fail you. That is man as in mankind. It is not humanly possible to be perfect, so every one of us come with flaws. You will even recognize that all the let downs are not intentional but inevitable; it is impossible for man not to fail. But God. It is impossible for God to fail. (Luke 1:37).

Like everything else, trusting God is a decision you must make for yourself. It can take many tests before you finally trust Him. Or you can truly trust Him from the start and later lose that trust when tests do come. Other times you can say and may possibly feel that you trust Him yet deep down it is not completely true. Remember Proverbs 3:5 says trust Him with all your heart. It does not say trust Him with only your finances, only your family, only the tip of your heart. You must be completely "souled" out. Give Him you whole self, your whole heart.

The verse also says do not lean on your own understanding. (Proverbs 3:5). We have a limited thinking as humans. You can have the highest IQ and be the smartest person in the class or office, yet there are limitations in humanity. If you lean on your own understanding, you are in the natural. In the natural you do not have enough money for the bills weekly, you are not good enough to receive God's love, or you do not truly know who you are yet. Praise God that He cannot be limited. He does not live in the natural; therefore, He does not move in the natural. The things God can and will do for you surpass all understanding; it will be exceedingly and abundantly what you can ask. (Ephesians 3:20).

When you finally stop trying to give all your trust to earthly things or people and give Him all your trust. How things begin to fall in place will shock you in the natural, but when you are leaning on Him you will be confident in knowing that those miraculous wonders were of God. Once you have given God your whole heart, He will show you how to trust others. You will not lean to the point of codependency, but you can and will functionally have other trusting relationships. It took my relationship with God to know what friends to trust, who to date, what job was best for me, when to move, how to handle difficult decisions, and where to invest my time and money.

After building my relationship with God and trusting Him wholeheartedly, I was getting confirmation from everywhere that He was with me. Sometimes God will move some things out of your way for you to see He is with you. You could possibly believe you are missing out on something when you're in the process. However, later God will reveal to you that it was all for your God. (Romans 8:28).

I know trust is hard. I know people you thought you could depend on have hurt you. I know you have been let down more times than you can remember. I also know God is faithful. Dare to trust Him and believe in Him. You are in for the time of your life.

I Need a Breakthrough before I Breakdown

*F*ollowing Christ is not always easy. In fact, for some, life gets harder than it ever was beforehand. While in the world, things could have come a lot easier. There were readily available resources nearby. Were these resources God's best? They absolutely were not. But it was convenient. When you finally decide to turn from the worldly resources you once heavily depended on, life comes at you fast.

I think back to a conversation I was having with a friend Patrice. I need to give a little background about her for it all to make sense. She is an only child. She was once a daddy's girl but after adolescence her dad married a woman who was not her mother, and she grew closer to her mom. She was very spoiled in a sense that her mom, grandparents, or male suiters we ready and willing to give her anything she wanted. Whenever she had an issue, Patrice knew she could pick up the phone and call someone to come to the rescue. Life was not the hardest for her because she had so many resources at her beckon call.

The Lord tugged on my friend Patrice's heart. She was tired of depending on others. She wanted to follow Christ. When Patrice made the conscious decision to do better with her life, she started getting hit in every way possible. I am telling you now, the devil will attack you hard when he knows you are ready to walk in God's purpose for your life. Her relationship with her boyfriend fell apart. Neither of her parents were dependable anymore. In fact, they were adding more stress by bringing their personal issues to her door, ruining her credit when she did try to help, and then coming in and out of her life when it was convenient for them. She was put out of her home because of situations beyond her control. Finances got so bad she had to take legal action. Patrice said to me, "Friend, my life is in shambles." She felt she should go back out in the world and do what she was doing before because at least she had a safe place to lay her head and food to eat. She knew that those people in her life wanted her to need them. If Patrice came back, they would help her but with a price. I encouraged her while praying with and for her. I listened thoroughly to her concerns. I knew the Lord was moving in her life. She just had to allow Him to fully prune her. I never tried to fix Patrice's situation. I needed my own help. I honestly had no answers and no options other than trying God. He had already revealed to me that He was in control.

My friend Patrice said she felt she was completely falling apart. She needed a breakthrough from God before she had a complete breakdown. She was at a point many of us have been before. She felt that The Lord had put too much on her. She was unable to bear all the hits she was receiving from life. Patrice was trying to stay faithful and refused to turn back to the life she left, but it looked so much more appetizing than what was in front of her at that given time.

What I learned from her situation and others like it: God WILL put more on you than you can bear. It is a mere myth when people say, 'He will not put more on you than you can bear.' I have yet to find that in the bible. In your flesh, there is not much you can bear. I mean you can be physically the strongest, fastest person on earth. Yet mentally and emotionally you still need to link into your source to get the job done. Sometimes God must all but break us before we are able to fully receive the breakthrough He is ready to bring to us. He wants us to know that no matter how bad things get we always have Him to turn to for help. There is nothing God cannot do. With

Him, all things are possible. Unfortunately, it can take a pure breakdown before we are ready to finally say, "Lord I cannot do this thing alone. Please help me. I need You. I realize I cannot do this on my own." And right before you feel your shoulders are about to explode with that load, God lifts it. Like Paul, we too should boast in our infirmities or weaknesses. (2 Corinthians 12:9). Praise God for His grace. As weak as my friend felt, God was working right then during it all.

Within months everything turned around for Patrice. A month before she graduated college, she got a new job in her field with a pay increase. She was able to move in her own home at a very reasonable cost. Her credit score was better than ever before. She did the work, and her relationships with her family strengthened. She sought counseling for herself. She knew that God had professionals to assist her with everything she was dealing with. She was able to process and heal from the inside out. Once her boyfriend saw how faithful God was to her it made him rededicate his life as well for his own healing and growth. Her faith walk showed him that if God could do it for her, God could also do it for him even if that meant them not being together. My friend Patrice got to the point of realizing she could not go back to the person she used to be, but she could also not handle all life had to dish out without her Heavenly Father fighting her battle.

I wish I could say that was the end of her battle. No, it did not end there. When you are a true child of God, the devil wants what you have. He wants to take all the good God has given you and make you use it for his will instead. And the devil continued to probe Patrice like he does us all. These instances were more subtle. When you pray for something and work for it, remember the devil hears those prayers as well. While Patrice was changing her life for the better, she began another relationship with someone who seemed to be an awesome person. Once they got deeper in, she learned he was not a man of God even though he proclaimed to be. She knew how she had prayed to God for his best in all areas of her life. After trying to work through things she finally said enough is enough. She called back on how God had got her through so much while she was at her lowest and knew He was still faithful. It is one thing to have a breakthrough while dating, but it is important to take those same principles God taught you through other areas of your life. She did just that. She continued to grow professionally and personally. While bumps and bruises come her way, Patrice refused to settle and is looking and doing amazing. Not settling for subpar because it is easy is an important lesson to remember. God will carry you through your breakdown to get you where He needs you to be and even after He will still be there with you.

Many of us are still struggling with those resources of the world or dealing with possible breakdowns. Know that what is in the world is not God's best for you. He has so much greater in store for His children. You must earnestly seek His face. (Psalm 27:8 NIV). God fights our battles, so we do not have to. That breakthrough is around the corner. You will not break down if you are in His will. He will not allow that to happen. Trust that the Lord takes care of His own. Whenever you are in a place where you feel you will break down if you do not receive a breakthrough soon, have faith that God will see you through it. Start praising and praying. Praise will surely confuse the enemy. Believe that it is already done. The victory will be that much sweeter when The Lord shows Himself faithful.

Likewise, I have a sister in Christ Michelle who was dealing with a similar situation. She informed us that she felt everything in her life was going wrong. Her career, her marriage, and her family were all taking hits. It was so much happening, and she was not sure how to handle everything. She was used to fixing her problems as well as the problems of the people around her. This was more difficult this time around.

Being a praying woman, Michelle went to her closet. This is not a physical closet. She went to the place where she could spread out before God without distraction. This was the one space Michelle's children had learned not to enter when Mommy was in there. She cried out to God letting Him know all that was happening in her life. She wanted Him to know she felt that her back was against the wall, and she had no other way to turn.

Instantly Michelle said the Lord spoke to her. He revealed to her that He is the wall her back is against. That touched me. Some people do not even have a wall to hold them up. I have been "some people" myself. Yes, her back was against the wall, but it is because God was still holding her up and would not let her fall. That is something to praise God about. His love is so strong, so powerful, it literally held her up. Imagine how things would have gone without that wall behind her. Exactly, it would have been utter chaos. But the Lord does not allow the bottom to fall out from behind His people without being our safety net.

If there is ever a time you feel backed into a corner, know that God will not allow you to fall without a plan already in place to get you back up better than ever. This does not mean you are exempt from God breaking you down to a point that there is no place to turn but to Him. However, no one will get the glory but God. He will ensure that. If it takes you going in the closet, the restroom, a stall, the hallway, get some alone time with God and pour your heart out to Him. Yes, He already knows what you are going through, but He desires to hear it from you. And He needs to know that you truly desire His help. He is that Breakthrough before you break down. He is that Wall when you are backed into a corner. He is Lord of lords and King of kings. (1 Timothy 6:15). He will not allow you to fall apart. You are His child; He loves you. Allow Him to move in your life.

Ch 5
Emotional Runner

$\mathcal{I}$ have dealt with many tragedies in my life. Some of my encounters were a little more difficult to deal with than others. I can remember a friend, or two, telling me when things get beyond what I can handle emotionally, I disappear. When I sat and thought about it, I realized it was true.

When Eli, the man I thought I would spend the rest of my life with, decided that I was not the one he wanted to spend the rest of his life with, I instantly shut down. I did not eat; I did not talk to any of my family or friends. I was completely isolated. I did not know how to deal with those emotions. I refused to be open about what I was dealing with emotionally with anyone. I did not pray about it. Pray? Ha! The last person I wanted to discuss this failure and heartbreak with was God. God knows all and sees all. He knew this would happen to me. He could have softened the blow but did not. I was absolutely not going to God with it. I tried to bury it deep inside. That was not the best idea. The hurt manifested in various ways physically and it was noticeable.

The same thing occurred when I was unsuccessful my first attempt on the bar exam. To be a licensed attorney, the final exam you must pass in the state bar exam. Exams vary, but they mostly focus on numerous areas of law through essay, multiple choice, and other ways of application. It is a two-day exam for most states, and some states even have a third day. After studying for months, I sat for the exam that would change the trajectory of my life. I was nervous. My mind was thinking of every what if scenario possible. Everybody was depending on me. I knew the law, but mentally I was not there. I received my bar results in an email. As soon as I saw that I was unsuccessful, my heart hit the floor. I cried so long and so hard I could not breathe. I locked myself in my room. I disconnected from social media and did not take calls, not even from my father. Failing the biggest exam of my life was too much to bear emotionally. Of course, I could not talk to God. He allowed me to fail, and I contemplated my worth as a result. I could not function. My days were the longest and the nights were darkness filled with the moistness from my tears going into my ears while I looked up in the direction of the ceiling but seeing nothing but black. Every time my face would dry up, a new batch of tears would come out of nowhere. However, I refused to tell anyone these things. I could not face the music.

It did not stop there. Whenever there was emotional pain I could not handle, I would try to mentally escape. I remember wanting to sleep until I could not feel any emotions. I even contemplated suicide. I mean why not? I did not know it at the time, but I was dealing with depression. And in my community depression was not openly discussed. We were told to take it to God and leave it there. Why do you need a therapist when you have Jesus? But Jesus was not there in the physical to help me work through all I was feeling. Also, Jesus allowed all this to happen to me in the first place. Jesus knew I was going to fail the bar exam. Jesus knew I was going to get my heartbroken. Jesus knew I was in for the hardest moments of my life. He did not stop them from coming. I literally had no one. Because I was not sure who I could talk to about the despondency, I ran from my emotions.

I thought that my emotions were sinking to the ground since I would not face them. My dysphoria stopped me from directly facing my emotions. It became sickening. I would not eat or communicate. I slept my way through it all. When I began socializing, I pretended everything was fine. I was good at it too. No one suspected a thing. We have all been let down in life and bounces back. I am sure everyone thought I was on my bounce back. However, with unresolved hurt and pain, I aggregated my own problems. I entertained relationships I would have never done so otherwise. The relationships were not successful, and I did not even want them to be in the first place. I excessively drank alcohol. It was more than socially at this point. I would be lying if I said I thought the answer to my problems was in that bottle. That was not the case at all. I simply did not want to face my reality and alcohol took me from my truth for a short period of time. But that too was unsuccessful.

I realized that amid running from my emotions I was also running from God. Of course, it is impossible to run from God. However, I was not praying as I should. During "prayer" I was lashing out due to my anger. I was telling God how "good" I am and that I did not deserve the hurt. I deserved to be loved, I deserved to be a lawyer. I deserved to have my dreams fulfilled. I would not meditate or wait for God to talk back to me. I did not honestly think God would say anything back. I was too focused on handling it myself, I was not truly seeking Christ. I wanted to feel like I was being a good Christian when I was not being authentic at all. I was projecting my anger without seeking God. I was throwing all these words out and had no idea where they were landing or if they were even landing. I even felt that I sought Christ in everything else, and it all resulted in failure. If my going to God with everything else resulted in so much pain, it was best I figured this out another way. Right?

We sometimes get to a point where we feel as though we have reached our limit. We refuse to do things how we did them in the past because it did not yield the exact result that we wanted. I quickly learned that being "good" did not mean I deserved anything. The wages of sin is death. (Romans 6:23A). However, I am thankful that the gift of God is eternal life in Christ Jesus our Lord.

(Romans 6:23B). It took all the disappointments for me to see that I was not above God's word. While things were not working out for me how I wanted them to work, they were working according to God's plan. (Romans 8:28). No matter what I did, God examined my heart. My heart was not with Him. God needed me to put my faith in Him instead of a relationship or a job. Sometimes for God to get you right where He needs you, He must remove those distractions. He must halt your plans to let you know that He is still in control.

It took God lining me up with a therapist to face myself. It was not easy. It was not fun. Peeling layers of pain back was excruciating. I realized why I ran from my emotions. They hurt. It is no other way to put it. The emotions were more painful than some physical pain I have endured. However, to be the person I was destined to be, I had to deal with the hurt. It was done gradually, over time. I told my therapist how I was an emotional cutter as a teen as my coping mechanism. Some professionals call it self-mutilation. It is the acts of deliberately harming your own body to cope with emotion pain, intense anger, and frustration. It was another way to run from my emotions. My therapist was the second person I told. The only other person was my ex-boyfriend. While in therapy I also learned of my codependency, but that is for another time. I was talking to my therapist, I was following up with homework, I was doing the work, I was healing. All this was in my late 20s. I was thinking to myself wow, I have been messed up for years. But there is no time like now. My therapist was skilled in this area. She provided positive coping mechanism and reminded me that I had many positive mechanisms I previously used before I began shutting down.

I would like to share some of those positive coping mechanisms. Please note, everyone is different. Use what works for you. This is not an exhausted list. I am by no means a therapist of any sort. However, I pray what I learned in my sessions can bless someone else.

1. Positive affirmation. These are quotes or saying specific to what you are dealing with that you want to recite at the beginning and end of your day. Some people even deem it helpful to post them in places you frequent to see them more often. If you have ever seen Being Mary Jane, this is something Gabrielle Union's character did very often.

2. Meditation. Clear your mind. We think about so much and our mind is wandering (and wondering) always. Try to center yourself and find peace and calmness. There are particularly useful apps on your smart phone for this. If using your phone will lead to you going to social media instead, do this without your phone. Get in tune with your body and find serenity.

3. Journaling. This is hands down my favorite. I have a prayer journal where I write to Jesus. I know I can pray to him, but it also brings me comfort and peace when I flip through the pages and remember what He helped me through. I can be as open and as honest as I want. So many things we do not feel comfortable telling others about. Write it out. You get it off your chest and no one else must know until you are ready to express those feelings.

4. Paint or color. Did you know coloring books for adults was a thing? I had no idea. I am not an artist by any means, but who does not want to create a great masterpiece? It requires attention to detail if you are coloring. If you decide to paint, you can be as raw as you want by putting it all on canvas. Michael's and other art stores have unbelievably cute small canvases that come with paint. While this can be done in a group, you may want to do this alone if you are using this as a coping mechanism.

5. Music or dance party. Play some of your favorite tunes. This does not have to be Christian or gospel. Whatever you listen to makes you feel better, put it on. Incorporate dance if you would like. Dance until you are laughing, tired, and ready to fall out. Start a play list or just let Pandora find the tunes for you. Set a timer for 15 to 30 minutes or if you are brave an hour. Be carefree and in the moment. Enjoy that time without thinking of the worries in the world.

The timeline varies for everyone. I originally went to see my therapist every week. I looked forward to seeing her although we dealt with complicated issues. It later went to twice a month. Apparently, I was making progress. For some, a monthly visit to handle the day-to-day issues is the best outlet. I have known others to do very intense every day for a period which was perfect for them. With the distractions removed and me being able to cope with my emotions, I realized my delay was not a denial. God said if it would have been easy for me, I would not have appreciated it. I would have taken the glory for myself. I can tell you when I did get my bar exam results after the second time, I cried out to God in the middle of a restaurant with my aunt. I had passed and it was nobody but God. I knew it was all Him. I was beyond ecstatic because I knew God had me covered and he had not forgotten about me. Remember how I refused to even talk to God about my hurt in the beginning, and in the end, He is all I wanted. He was my help, and I knew it.

No more running from myself. I have now learned to face my emotions. I can say that I still do not handle them how others do. However, I make sure I am doing what is best for me. I am not holding things in, but I am discussing things in a respectful manner. I pray about everything. If God does not speak, I will not move. I learned to wait for His answer instead of prematurely jumping to my own conclusion. Waiting, no matter how long it takes. I used to be the most nonchalant when it came to certain situations because I was unable to emotionally process it. Now, I process through journaling and prayer. God has made me emotionally available, and it is liberating. I do not always have the words. I wait on God to give them to me. Even when He does not give me words, He gives me peace. And that is an amazing gift.

Ch 6
Faith over Fear

The Bible says so many times do not be afraid. It is because the Lord knows how strong the spirit of fear is. Fear tactics are used today from the media, politicians, employers, and anyone else who wants to scare you into doing what they would have you to do. Fear is an immensely powerful spirit that Satan uses to stop us from reaching our purpose in life through Christ. The devil wants to simply halt us in any manner he can, and he desires to be in control. Do not give him that power over you; only God is in control.

I think about all the things I have feared in my lifetime. It may sound minor, but I was afraid of the dark well into adulthood. But being afraid of the dark crippled me in many ways. There were times when I was extremely parched but depending on if there was light for me to see my way to the kitchen I may or may not get up to get a drink a water. Fast forward to being an adult, no light was still affecting me. I would have fears of someone coming in my place to attack me if I did not have some sort of nightlight on. I finally had no choice but to sleep in the dark once I got in apartment where my bedroom had no windows. Yes, it was an actual bedroom with a closet I could have rented out as a third bedroom. However, my room had no windows. I got some of the best sleep in the world. I am still grateful my roommate wanted the room with the ensuite bathroom. Even friends would come over, they would oversleep because it got so dark. They literally had no idea the sun was out, and they got some much-needed rest. Since then, sleeping in the dark is now my preference and I love it.

Then we have the fear of driving over bridges of water, or gephyrophobia. This fear is very paralyzing. Think about not being able to cross over some states because there are bridges of water that separate the states or municipalities. I can recall a visit to my law school one summer. My uncle, being a truck driver, told me the route to take. I asked if I would have to cross any water. He warned me about the Ohio River. Instantly I was afraid. My heart began to race, I could feel the steam from heat under my clothes. I had a nervous sweat I had never felt. Fear was manifesting in the physical. I considered pretending that I went up to that law school for a week all while staying at my friend's apartment which was only twenty minutes away from my place. I had it all planned out. I would camp out at the apartment, cook breakfast, lunch, and dinner, as my payment to get the couch for an entire week. Also, it was to make sure my secret was safe because I did not want a soul to know I was considering skipping out on law school because of my fear of bridges. I needed to be delivered from myself, seriously. My fear of driving over bridges was about to stand in the way of my legal career.

However, God is stronger. Fear will block and stop so many things. Satan will sit back pleased that you did not allow your blessings to move forward. God said do not be afraid because He is with you. (Isaiah 41:10). He is with all of us. The Bible states "fear not" 365 times. That is a "fear not" for every day of the year. When I am afraid, I put my trust in you. (Psalm 56:3). This is what we all must do. Although fear is part of being human, we cannot live in that fear. We cannot let fear control us and keep us away from what God has for us. Whenever fear tries to rise up in your spirit, instantly bind that emotion. Say a prayer to the Lord letting Him know you trust Him. Be open and honest. Let the Lord know that you are afraid, but you do not want this fear to consume you. You can also call His Word back out to Him. Consider this prayer or some variation of it:

Father God, I love You and trust You. I come to You right now because the fear of _____ has risen in my spirit. I know Your Word says that You have not given us the spirit of fear (2 Timothy 1:7) therefore I know this fear I am feeling is not of You. I bind the feeling of fear that is preventing me from getting what You desire for me. I send that feeling back to hell where it belongs. You are with me Lord, and I will not be afraid (Psalm 118:6). Lord, I thank You for being my light, salvation, and the stronghold of my life (Psalm 27:1) You are such a great God. I thank You for Your angels that are encamped around me (Psalm 34:7). I know I will be victorious because I have You. Thank you for releasing the spirit of fear off me completely. This and all things I pray in Your wonderful Son's Jesus' name. Amen.

I thank God that He gave me the courage to drive over the bridge crossing the Ohio River. Through the anxiety, sweat, and tears, I made it. Because the devil did not win, I crossed the bridge and safely arrived at my law school where I completed an intense weeklong conditional program for me to be considered for acceptance into the law school. Not only did I cross the bridge going there, but I also had to cross the bridge coming back. I wish I could tell you that it was not as scary. That would be a complete fabrication of my reality. It was still very scary, but I knew it was necessary. I even considered other ways and they would still have me crossing bodies of water unless I was willing to drive double the time. I had to think back on God getting me across the bridge the first time. He had to do it again because He is God. I also knew that God was riding with me and there is no way He was going to let me down at this point or ever. Because I did not allow fear to keep me away from that visit to my law school, I was accepted to start at the next available class. I graduated from this very law school, and now I am a practicing attorney. Think about what could have been the outcome had I let the devil win. I thank God I never have to know what it would have been like not to cross over that bridge because my faith was rooted in Him.

Fear is of the flesh. I know we all have stories where fear has gotten in the way of true wants and desires for ourselves. Fear may have even stopped us from doing something God has told us to do. And since I am being honest, I will tell you now, fear has staying power. I refuse to say the fear will go away, that there was a magic wand to wipe away every fear. That is not how it works. Even in fear, you must press forward. Even when you are afraid, you must act. When you know this is truly God's will for your life, do not let your flesh halt you. This does not mean if you were afraid to reach out to your abusive ex that I am telling you to act and see if he or she has now changed. Absolutely not. This does not mean I am saying it is okay to leave a job that God has not given you the okay to leave. You must know when God is speaking. You must know when He has ordered your steps. Do not ignore God or give up on your journey with God because of the fear of your flesh.

A way to move forward is to thank Him and praise Him in the process. Be real with God. *Lord, I am afraid. I know you want me to start that business, but this corporate position is safe. Lord, I know you want me to be healthy, but I am afraid of people making fun of me at the gym. I do not know where to start. Lord, I am scared. Your Word says You are with me, but I feel alone. Help me Father. I know this is your will for my life. I refuse to let my fear win over my Father.*

Transparency goes a long way. Think about all the times you have asked someone to simply be real and say how they feel so you do not have to guess. Well, our heavenly Father sometimes want you to be open and honest about where you are. Try it with Jesus. Watch Him order your steps to overcome those fears of the flesh. Instead of fearful to the point of not fulfilling God's desire for you, turn that fear into something healthy. Healthy fear is when you are still mobile, and you refuse to be paralyzed. Esther was fearful when her cousin Mordecai told her maybe she was queen for such a time as this so that their people were not killed off. (Esther 4:14). Peter was scared when Jesus told him to walk on water. (Matthew 14:29). I know you do not think Daniel was completely fearless when he heard he could possibly be thrown in the lion's den. (Daniel 6). Do not let that fear stop God from getting the glory through you. Who knows, it could be the start or cherry on top of something amazing. Romans says the mind governed by the flesh is death, but the mind governed by the Spirit is life and peace. (Romans 8:6 NIV). I am not trying to tell you to be fearless. I am saying even in fear, do it. Do not let fear govern your mind, body, or spirit. I choose life and peace. What about you?

Pray Before Not After

I can think back on so many good and bad times in my life. A lot of those times involved my high school sweetheart. He was such a hunk. Well, he was to me for several years. From the time I met him, even before I liked him, he was the most attractive man in the world to me. Once we got to know each other, I realized I was right. Tall, chocolate, slender basketball build, with a smile that literally made me smile. Even in his "my way or the highway" mentality, he was still so fine I was like okay I guess it's your way because no way it's the highway for me. That did not stop us from arguing and having so many disagreements. I would grow so angry at him that I knew I could no longer be with this man. So, I would call it off. I broke up with him more times than I can count because I was emotionally unstable. When I snapped back to reality, I could not believe what I had done. I had ended things with my man over the smallest thing (usually having to do with him not buying me food or him wanting food I did not want). After that, I would pray to God to please give me my whole man back. My pet name for him was my whole man. And he lived up to that for the most part. Even still, I would click out on him at any given point when I did not get my way. I know I overreacted, I know I acted on my emotions, I know I was wrong. If the Lord could just give me my man back after all the crazy things I had done and said, I would not do or say those crazy things again.

Of course, that was a vicious cycle that went on for year, almost ten years. I was not being led by the Holy Spirit at all. I was being led by my emotions only. I truly felt like this was the person I was supposed to love for life, marry, and have babies with. We all have that person and persons in our past (in some instants present) that we honestly thought was "the one". We plan our lives around the person. We make decisions based on what we think that person would want or think. But what about what God wants from us? To love the Lord your God with all your heart and with all your mind and with all your strength, is what Jesus wants from us. (Mark 12:30 NIV). It is not to give another person so much power in your life that the person becomes your idol or god. I realize today that this relationship was an unhealthy type of love. Yes, he had great qualities. He was the tall, dark, and handsome man that women wanted plus he was smart, funny, a leader, and a provider. I did not ask God prior. I basically decided this man is my husband and later told God to make it happen time and time again. God was probably so sick of me. He was thinking my child is so lost she has no idea what is best for her. My whole man was that dude with a laundry list of amazing qualities, but he lacked something. There were no God qualities. He was not a follower of Christ. At the time, I was not fully walking in God's will so I believed that this man being a good guy would be good enough. But we deserve more than *good enough*. We deserve God's best. One thing that exemplifies a person is God's best is to see God in that person's life.

By no means do I want you to think that God's best is dressed in white gliding down the church aisle ready to take you by the hand and pray the demons out of you. The person God's has for you looks different for each of us. Only you know you. I will not put the specifics I desired from a man in you. All I know is, just having a "good heart" is not always enough. You will see that God's best has something that stands out no matter how subtle it is. You will see through a different lens and think this was nobody but God. While that whole man of mine did not exemplify any type of relationship with God, I felt I could make him have this relationship. You are either thinking *wow she really was crazy*, or you are thinking *so that is not a thing I can do?* Yes, I was crazy and no that is not something we can do. We are not Jesus no matter how tight we are with Him. I was completely wrong. I had a messianic complex thinking that 1) I could love him so much he would see God's love in me; 2) I could persuade him to go to church that would hopefully result in him having a personal relationship with God; and 3) he would see my relationship with God and want that for himself.

I had to come to the reality that I cannot save anyone. I am only human. I have my own flaws, demons, sins, and I did not die on the cross for humanity. Jesus is our Lord and Savior. He is the Messiah. I was going about this thing all wrong. I should not have thought that I was in the position to get anyone to heaven. Honestly, this man whom I loved seeing me as a Christian saying I love God but putting more faith in him than the One True God at times was possibly one of the most damaging things I could have done. I wanted him to go to church only because I was going. It looked like the good Christian religious thing to do. So other people could see us in church together. I had gotten to the point that his relationship with God was not even a major issue any longer. I was so wrapped up in the image of us being in church as a couple, I was not focused on spiritual growth. And how could I be? Although I was the person wanting him to know God, I was the same person he was bedding whenever he desired. I had even gotten to the low point of withholding when he would not attend church service. In those instances, he only attended church because of his physical desire to be with me, not to be closer to God. I look back at this embarrassed with myself.

I later learned my messianic complex said more about me than it did about him. At no point did I look to God for guidance. I feared praying to God about certain things involving my relationship because I was always convicted. God was probably thinking *girl stop skirting around the real issue. You know what you are doing.* Because of this, I was a very strategic prayer. I prayed for so many other things and so many other people. When it came to praying for my relationship, almost the entire time we were together, I skipped that prayer altogether. I told myself I did not need to pray for myself all the time. It was more important to pray for others and show my love for others that way. It was all an excuse. I truly felt if I sought prayer in this area, God would chastise me. I was not ready for that. And worse. He would tell me to leave. And I was not about that life. I was in it to win it. This was my future forever. I knew that God disciplined those He loved, but I also was not ready to face Him. (Hebrews 12:6). I failed my then boyfriend Eli, myself, and God in so many areas at that time.

1. No amount of love for a man will make him do something he is truly not ready to do.

We are notorious for thinking we can make someone change. While I loved this man, and he loved me, I was the only person in that relationship who genuinely loved God. My love for my whole man did not make him inquiry about God's love. He may have even thought to himself, *if she really loves God how she says she does, she should walk out His Word. She is just like the rest of us.* I have heard men and women alike say they can change an individual and some have even gloated that they have already made an individual change. I am here to tell you that change is incited from within. (Ephesians 4:22-24). The God in me, the Holy Spirit residing in me, is what caused me to change for the better and grow. No human can truly have that impact on another. That would only be temporary and sooner or later you will see that person's true colors.

2. People must truly desire to have their own experience with Christ.

No amount of conversion was going to make this man experience Christ. My worldly tactics were definitely not going to assist in him growing in Christ. They may have even swayed him further away. For that, I pray for God's forgiveness. Even the times he did finally give in and attend church service, he was there to critique everything and everyone. He was there in the physical, but mentally and spiritually he had not opened his heart to receive Christ. No number of sexual favors could change that. I think back to King Nebuchadnezzar in the book of Daniel. He was a great, wealthy, and powerful Babylonian king. Daniel had interpreted his dreams and informed him that while he did such it was God and not him. King Nebuchadnezzar proclaimed that God was the One True God, but he did not live his life accordingly. While Daniel knew God for himself, King Nebuchadnezzar had yet to get that personal encounter. He still had gold statutes built to be worshipped. He continued to live for himself and not for God even after knowing God had rescued the three Hebrew boys from the fiery furnace. After yet another dream was interrupted by Daniel, it took that dream being fulfilled where King Nebuchadnezzar lost his entire kingdom and lived in the wild like an animal for him to raise his eyes toward heaven. In the wilderness he experienced God for himself. Only then was King Nebuchadnezzar truly ready to humble himself enough to follow God. (Daniel 2-4). Once he gained his own experience with the One True God, he undoubtedly knew that God was real. In our own wilderness is usually where we experience God for ourselves. My wilderness will not look like yours, but in it you will undoubtedly find God.

3. My relationship with God was bleak.

I was a believer who loved God, but I did not exemplify that love when I needed to do so most. I knew God loved me because he did everything to show me. (John 3:16). Yet, in return, I could not think of anything I outwardly expressed that was evident of my love for Him. No matter how kind and loving I was, my relationship with God was not appealing. I would scream how much I loved my man to the rooftop, but when it came time to proclaim Christ, I was one of the ones saying, "It doesn't take all that." In retrospect, my relationship with God was not evident. God asked Peter three times if he loved Him. (John 21). God could have asked me 100 times. Of course, yes would have been my answer every time because it was the truth. Yet there was not enough evidence of that love. According to John 21, God wants us to pour His Word into others. He wants us to follow Him. I missed the mark on both ends because I was not willing to pray to God first. I purposely chose not to strengthen my vertical relationship because of my obsession with my horizontal relationship. In the end, my own relationship with God was falling by the wayside so it could not have been a model for anyone else.

***

However, I never pondered about that man in my life. That was my whole man Eli, and I was going to stick beside him. I was in love with what I believe was a good man, and he was going to be my husband. It did not matter that at the time he would say to me, "Princess, I do not want to be married. It is not a priority to me. But, if I do decide to marry, it would be to you." The last part gave me hope. If I were smart, I would have run for the hills after that first time he expressed that to me. I would have even got on my face and asked God for guidance. But I did not. I wanted what I wanted so I had no real impetus. I was appeased for the moment. That if was giving me hope and that was enough for me.

From The Crushing to The Crown

In many instances, I postponed prayer until the storm was at my door. Not only did I wait until the storm was imminent, but I still did also not seek what God truly had for me. I was not ready to succumb to His ways. I was in panic mood. In instances where Jesus was in the middle of a storm, He was calm. So calm, that He was able to sleep peacefully. (Luke 8:22-25). When things got rocky in my relationship, I did not pray God's will or His peace. I prayed God give me what I wanted even if it meant chaos. When my friends and I disagreed, I did not pray we all come to a common ground and do what was best for the group. I prayed that they all saw things my way so I could get what I wanted. When grades were slipping in college, I did not pray for better time management to study, I begged for an A when I know I had not spent any time attempting to earn that grade. Knowing I had numerous tasks to complete for the week, I would do nothing and wait until the last minute and ask God to work a miracle. He was the miracle worker, not me.

It was not until I took the time to pray to God often, that I started seeing things change for the better. I prayed not only in the storm, but I prayed because I simply wanted to commune with God. I wanted to spend time with Him more than anyone else. I was very intentional about my time with God. I knew if I had three free hours after work, I could not waste it on social media or catching up on shows. I had to strategically carve out time for God. Exercise is especially important to me. I spend numerous days in the gym a week. I can admit I had days where my gym time would rollover and interrupt my time with God. While going to the gym meant not having as much time with God, it was okay to have that balance because I already built that relationship. I was literally calling on God in the middle of my workouts. The relationship I have with cardio, Jesus was the only way I could finish. I even incorporated Christian rap during my workout routines. Sometimes it can be very productive. Having the balance and intentionality is key. That is even more reason to pen specific time with God and stick with it. After work, meetings, the gym, time with family and friends, running errands, and chores, it may not feel like there is time in the day for God. You can still make the time. Something as simple as playing worship music while you are getting ready for work and having a five-minute uninterrupted conversation with God can be the best start to your day. During a lunch break or time to yourself, instead of checking your messages or emails, get a prayer up to God. If you do not get enough time alone, it could be easier to journal that prayer. God is listening to your heart.

Now that I know to pray before, during, and after the storm, I see how Jesus was able to have peace in the middle of the storm. Through prayer, I have learned that only one's own desire aligned with that of God's can change that person at their core. When I know people have yet to have a true moment with our Savior, I now pray and ask God that the individual gains that experience and that the person's heart and mind are open to receive Him. I had to strengthen my own relationship with God by increasing communication. (1 Thessalonians 5:17). Talking with Him every day allowed that relationship to grow. I no longer look to my pastor's relationship with God, my mom's relationship with God. I have my own and it is delightful. Yes, I still seek wise counsel. I still attend church. However, as much as I wish it could, I know someone else's relationship with God cannot give me the closeness I desire with God. I cannot watch other people workout and eat right then expect to lose weight. I must put in my own work. We all must have that personal relationship. I pray that we all gain a personal relationship with Christ and learn to foster that relationship constantly. You can sometimes let what is happening in the world pull you away. If you think prayer always must be isolated, take it from me, that is not the case. I pray in the grocery store. I pray in the car. I pray at the nail salon and beauty shop. By any means necessary, I will commune with God. I talk to God like I talk to my girls because He is my friend. I do not change my diction. He made me, so God knows exactly how I talk. I enjoy the relief of being my true self with Him. Now, I seek Him out always. I am not trying to plan everything myself then add God in later. I go to God, wait for an answer, and wait, and wait, until I know I am moving how He wants me to move. It is not easy. I want to give in at times, but I trust God. I love the relationship we have because I do not want to hurt Him. I am all in and not willing to compromise that intimacy with Him. This was not always the case and was a true process. This process looks different for everyone and even in the end the relationship you have with God can be inseparable, it will still look different from mine. Thank God for the uniqueness in all of us and the unique relationships He has with us.

Ch 8
Damaged Goods
vs
Complete Waste of a Woman

*B*e *careful what you allow into your ear-gates and eye-gates. Do not answer to anything. Make sure you know who you are in Christ.* These statements stuck with me although I did not always abide by them. Let me be open and honest. I was not always saved. Complete shocker, right? It should not be because most of us have a past. In my past, I did not always live the life God set out for me. Many times, I was wrapped up into what I wanted, and it was in total disregard for my Lord Jesus Christ. While I was in the world, I was befriending and dealing with people who were also in the world. My friends are great people. However, we felt we were young and wanted to live life with no regrets. We did not always make the best decisions because we wanted to make memories. Why would I want to purposely befriend those who would encourage me to do things Christ-like when that was not the life I was trying to live at the time?

I want to give a slight disclaimer. What you are about to read are not kind words. These are words I was told about myself. These may even be words we have said to each other unfortunately. I do not condone these words at all. I know I needed to touch on this specific topic because it is so important. Words can heal and they can harm. These words harmed me because I allowed them to do so. I was beyond hurt, but I grew. I advise you to read this in hopes that this gets you through. However, if harsh words are too much for you, you may want to skip this chapter.

I have spoken about my high school sweetheart to you before. He was my whole man. We had been together since I was six-teen years old. I knew then he was the man I would marry. I thought I knew a lot at the time. We applied to one of the same colleges. We both got accepted; we both attended. While in college we were a whirlwind, but I had no doubt he was my future husband after all, he was mine and I was sticking beside him. I had never in my life felt so strongly about anything before. Therefore, I coined the nickname of my whole man just for him. After college we lived in separate areas of the country both following dreams of our own. He moved further South to Atlanta, Georgia. I moved to the Midwest, the center of the boot, Lansing, Michigan. He and my uncle and his friends had so kindly moved me the 12 hours from Memphis to Lansing. We had a short conversation while he was still in Lansing. I remember at the door before he left me to go back South, he told me that our love could withstand anything, and he reassured me this would grow us closer together. He believed distance makes the heart grow funder. I was all in. He loved me. I loved him.

Well let me fast forward to my second year in the Midwest because things started to take a sharp turn with me and the whole man. We had so many struggles I felt that world was falling apart. We both started to date other people. We both got serious with other people. He and I drifted apart, but still tried to hold on to our history and memories. One day via social media, my whole man found out I was seeing another man romantically. He called and we argued while I was dining with that guy. Yes, in the middle of my crepes in Detroit, I saw who was calling, excused myself, and walked out the restaurant. At that time in my life, no one could have made me not answer. I could have been standing in line at the pearly gates waiting to get in, and if my cellphone rang My Whole Man, I was going to answer the call on the first ring. Heaven understood. On the other end of the phone, my whole man was very unhappy and disgusted with me. He articulated his point very well while all I could say was, "But you are doing the same thing." And he was. The other reason I had even done a quarter of the things I had done is because I learned of all the things he had done while back in Memphis. I do not remember all the words that were said, but I remember he said to me, "You are damaged goods now and I will never want you again." That stood out and stuck with me. Those words pierced my heart like a dagger. I went back to my crepes and date dead inside.

People will have you thinking that words are nothing. Even as children we say words could never hurt us. The saying, "Sticks and stones may break my bone, but words can never hurt me," is something we all remember reciting during childhood, Some, maybe even recently. Well, those hurtful words from someone I confided in rang louder than any other words I had ever heard. I am not sure if this were because I felt as if he may have been right or because I knew from that point forward, the whole man and I would never be again. Either way, those words were in my mental and I felt them as if they were a part of me. *Be careful what you allow into your ear-gates and eye-gates. Do not answer to anything. Make sure you know who you are in Christ.* Every word after that, I have no recollection. All of it went out the window because I was at an all-time low. The person I was supposed to grow old and die with felt I was nothing but damaged goods. I previously had so much hope for us, but at that moment I felt like nothing. My spirit had been broken.

For anyone who has had their spirit broken, at that time you do not feel like you will ever grow from there. You are not sure you will truly ever be okay. I am here to tell you my friends, it gets better. That happened to me almost a decade ago. I can tell you today I am not damaged goods. Jesus does not put words in your heart and spirit for nothing. Let me tell you what got me out of that low place, and what will stop you from ever going there. If you have been there before, it will ensure you do not go again. If you are still in that place, it will surely get you out.

Be careful what you allow into your ear-gates and eye-gates.

Philippians 4:7-8 NIV reads, "And the peace of God, which transcends all understanding, will guard your hearts and your minds in Jesus Christ. Finally, brothers and sisters, whatever is true, whatever is noble, whatever is right, whatever is pure, whatever is lovely, whatever is admirable—if anything is excellent or praiseworthy—think of those things."

There are two parts to this. We must allow God to act first. Then we must do our part. This is a bilateral contract. The word says the peace of God will transcend all understanding and guard your heart. That means, God will block such words from ever getting to you. While the world is watching Love and Hip Hop or the Kardashians, God may tell you to turn the TV off and get in His word. While the world is listening to Cardi B or Meg thee Stallion, God may tell you that you have had enough of that for now, tune in to Hillsong or Tamela Mann. The Lord will place on your heart what He does not want you to be involved in; He will also place on your heart what He does want you to be involved in.

The second part is on you. God gives you a blueprint in Philippians 4:8 as to what you should have your mind on. If it is not true, noble, right, pure, lovely, admirable, excellent, or praiseworthy is it really of God? We must be careful not to listen or watch things that are contradictory of this blueprint from God. This means cutting that conversation short with your best friend who only wants to gossip. This means not listening to misogynistic lyrics from your favorite band's or artist's new song you want to support. It could even mean not returning the family members call until you have mentally prepared to nicely end the call when it goes into trash talking any and everybody.

God has promised He will guard our hearts. However, we must want our hearts to be guarded. I spoke up and was honest that I was not ready to fully receive Christ at one point. Only you and God know when you are truly ready. It cannot be forced. But when I was ready those same words that I had already been taught finally had great meaning in my life. God's guarding of our hearts is ongoing. Once we fully accept it, we must continue to do our part. If God is convicting you on a show, an artist, a friend, or even a family member, know that is for a reason. Do your part and surround yourself with things that God deems worthy. This does not mean that you must turn down brunch invites with those who do not think like you. It also does not mean you cannot sit on a patio or watch a game with that gossiping friend. But you can learn to navigate the conversation. When people want to gossip, I am quick to say, "Whew chile, all I can do is pray because you never know what people are dealing with." This ends that conversation and allows time to discuss something new and refreshing. Other times, God will tell you when it is time to limit or eliminate contact with those who simply are not for you. He does a good job at removing them out of our lives. It is usually us holding on too long. Pray about it and seek guidance. I am a firm believer that we do not have to believe all the same things to enjoy each other's company and I can probably still learn from you. I am also a firm believer in letting go of anything that is dead and not growing or adding to your growth.

Do not answer to anything.

These few words are so powerful. God has given us a name. Because our Father has named us, as His children, we cannot answer to anything. The Lord paved the way for others to also follow His lead.

Jeremiah 1:5 ESV says, "Before I formed you in the

womb I knew you, and before you were born, I consecrated you." God thought so much of you that He already knew you before you were ever conceived. Before you were a twinkle in your parents' eyes God had already blessed you. He knew who you would be, and that person is victorious.

Moreover, John 10:3 ESV reads, "The sheep hear his voice, and he calls his own sheep by name and lead them out." I praise and thank God that He calls me by my name. He does not confuse me with my sisters or my coworkers; He specifically knows me and calls me personally by my name. When you are truly allowing God to lead you, you know His voice when He calls you. You know how special you are to Christ and that He will always be there to guide you. Psalm tells us that God will lead us. (Psalm 23:2). For us to follow Him he is not calling us unpleasant names, or names that make us question our being in Christ. God is also not calling us by titles or names acquired of multiple scholastic degrees or from various roles or positions.

If our God thinks highly enough of us to call us by our names, that should be the standard. It is not a suggestion that we are called by our names. God has already set the standard that must be followed by all. Even if your name is harder to pronounce, correct them. If your name is one like mine and people are in total disbelief, make sure they say it correctly. I refuse to answer to Precious, Peaches, damaged good, or anything else God does not call me. After all, He knew our names before we even knew ourselves. Inform others to put some respect on your name. It is, after all, a gift from God.

Make sure you know who you are in Christ.

So many people are quick to say they know who they are in Christ, but deep down they are not completely sure they really know who they are. And if they are sure, they are not living in it. I know because I have been "people" many times. When I get out of character any given day, I can be people again. It is okay to not know because it gives you a starting point. Praise God for the Word because it breaks it down completely and you will never have to question your existence in God again. When you are sure of who you are in Christ, you are confident that no one can shake up that relationship.

If you doubt, or have ever doubted, who you are in Christ, go to 1 Peter 2:9. The Word proclaims that you are a chosen generation, a royal priesthood, a holy nation, His own special people, that you may proclaim the praises of Him who called you out of darkness into His marvelous light. NKJV. Let me break this down to you. You are chosen. God chose you specifically. You are royalty. Because you are part of the lineage of Christ, you were born into the true royal family. You are holy. This has nothing to do with anything you did or did not do. Because of His hand on your life, you are righteous in Christ. You are special. You are different a set apart because of who you are in Christ.

Also, look to 2 Corinthians 5:17 which states that you if anyone is new in Christ, he is a new creation; old things have passed away; behold, all things have become new. NKJV. You are not the person you were when you were in the world. You are not the person you were last year and possibly not even last month. You may have gone through a dark period, but once you are in Christ, you are now in the light. Praise God that the person you used to be in now in the past and no one can hold that person over your head. Jesus has proclaimed you are a new creation. This does not mean life will be perfect. It also does not mean you will not look the same on the outside. But that God given joy that only comes from Him will be within you. It will show from the outside and you will glow of His goodness. Because of this you simply navigate situations differently. This is You walking in who you are in God.

And you better walk, walk, walk.

In Christ, you are everything good and perfect. You are marvelous. That is because God is with you, and He is the good, perfect, marvelous God. Never let what someone else thinks you are interject with what you know you are in Christ. His Word is extremely specific. I am not saying be nasty and mean to people and say this is just who I am in Christ. Do not use God as a stumbling block. God grows us. We all have ways that are not the best and in Christ we want to work on those while exemplifying Christ-like ways.

With this, you would think because you know these key things about your ear and eye gates, what you answer to, and who you are in Christ, you never have to worry about anyone ever trying to use words to get to you. Unfortunately, that is not the case. The Word says you will be hated by everyone because of [Jesus]. (Matthew 10:22 NIV). This means that now, even more than before, people will do their best to tear you down. I have already become victim of this more times than I want to admit. And sadly, it is from those you love.

In one instinct a particularly good male friend of mine wanted to tell me how he felt about my new relationship with Christ. Daryl is a jokester, so he wanted to make me his comic relief per usual. He informed me that he felt I was a waste of a woman for desiring to wait until I was married to have relations. Well, when I heard that, for a minute, I went back to what Eli had told me four years prior. In complete transparency it was for sure a trigger. I remembered the place I was in at that time four years earlier. I was so low, and my soul ached when I heard those words. I knew that I was no longer in that place, and I was thankful. God brought me out of that place stronger because he knew even on this side that I would be ridiculed because of my solidarity to Him. I now had my key phrases embedded in my heart at that point. *Be careful what you allow into your ear-gates and eye-gates. Do not answer to anything. Make sure you know who you are in Christ.*

I informed Daryl that I was sorry he felt that way. While he thought I was wasting my womanhood I know that I was doing exactly what God had told me to do. I no longer cared what people thought around me. I was secure in Christ and the little jabs at me that used to sting badly were no longer efficient. I was bold in my faith and let him know where I stood.

Daryl laughed off his comment, but he never made comments like that to me again. It would not be him not to joke on me, but his jokes began consisting of me being holy and special and always wanting to fellowship. I could now laugh with him. I can say for certain Daryl had no knowledge of my triggers, and he also had no idea that the Lord had already told me those things and because of that his words did not offend me, but they made me smile as I felt comforted by the Holy Spirit in that very moment. When someone tries to attack your character for simply living for Christ, never let that stop you from following God. Use that as ammunition to fuel your fire for Christ. When people see God on you, they will not always like what they see for various reasons. Some are dealing with their own battles, some are being convicted, and others could not even know God on a personal level. All places you and I may have been before. It is not up to us to figure out why they have a problem with the good in you. It is at that moment time for us to stand in our holiness and continue to glorify His Kingdom and remember all the grace God has given us we should also give.

When I was not living for God, I was considered damaged goods. When I became completed sold out for Christ, I was called a waste of a woman. Do not be alarmed because similar things will occur with you. Stand in what you believe in God. If you need to review and meditate on the scriptures previously mentioned, please do so. Whatever it takes, remember that if it does not line up with what the Lord has revealed to you, it is false. Period. And never forget: *Be careful what you allow into your ear-gates and eye-gates. Do not answer to anything. Make sure you know who you are in Christ.*

Ch 9
Forever Becoming

I gave myself a life mantra a few of years ago. Being completely honest, I borrowed it from someone I met on Twitter. I told myself I would go through life knowing that I was "Forever becoming." Knowing this meant living it as well. Instead of letting a storm in the clouds darken my day, I knew that if I could make it through the storm, it meant God was not done with me after all.

Being confident of this, that he who began a good work in you will carry it on to completion until the day of Christ Jesus (Philippians 1:6 NIV). God is not finished with you yet. Wherever you are in life at this moment, know that God is still working on you. You can be at an entry level position or the CEO, there is still growing to do. You can be struggling in a subject or making perfect scores in every current course, but God has even more in store for you. Maybe you just had to deal with the death of a loved one or the death of a relationship or friendship, God said you have not reached your mark just yet.

I came to a point in my life where I needed the Lord to work on my finances. I was doing enough to be considered okay, but I had been through some dead times. I did not want to get back to that point. I remember while studying for the bar exam I was a server and a barista while staying in my friend's extra room. After quitting the job as a barista, I lost my job as a server. I had already committed to moving into an apartment with my roommate the weekend after I passed the bar exam. While happy I was soon to be a licensed attorney, I was jobless and embarking on even more bills I had before. God worked it out for me. He provided. I am so thankful for the support I had, and how kind my roommate was to me knowing my situation. I know she was frustrated, but she was always there. I was asking for financial break-throughs. I was licensed so I started taking clients back home in Memphis from referrals. I was also doing contract work in Nashville and Charlotte as much as I could. Nothing was steady, and it was sort of eat what you kill lifestyle. I was only getting paid from clients I found or short-lived contract jobs. I was not complaining. I knew God was working things out and in due time I would be on the other side laughing about my current situation. At that time, all I could do was trust and try to make the absolute best decisions I could financially knowing I was only doing temporary work. His Word says my God shall supply all your need according to His riches in glory by Christ Jesus. (Philippians 4:19 NKJV).

There was no doubt in my mind the Lord would guide me. I realized if I wanted to be able to become who God desired me to become, I would need to be a good steward of all the things He provided to me. One of those things was the money I was receiving when I did have steady income. I knew it was not going to come over night. The Lord strategically placed solutions in front of my face. He provided me with the tools I needed to become what He desired. I am thankful that my bishop's book club included reading Dave Ramsey's The Legacy Journey. This book was extremely powerful, and it helped me in so many ways figure out how I needed to manage my funds and pay off debt. I recommend it to anyone. As my financial journey progressed the Lord also revealed to me different people who had gotten their finances in order. Everyone the Lord presented to me used biblical principles to get to the place God intended for them to be. I used many of the tips those peopled provided to progress financially. The Lord also put on my heart to reach out to a professional to assist with building my credit. I followed His lead. I am grateful and blessed to have a best friend whose passion is credit repair. She informed me ways to build my credit and different techniques I needed to use to maintain my high credit score. I was always taught to only pay in cash for everything. If you cannot pay it in cash, you do not need it. While that is a great lesson in theory, put it on a credit card and then use that cash to pay off the credit card. Still only spending what you know you can afford but growing your credit when you need to make large financial decisions like getting a car loan, business loan, or a home loan.

The Word is also the best source regarding finances. If you are from the South like me, you may have heard "there is more than one way to skin a cat." That is another way of saying there are multiple ways to reach the same result. However, when it comes to becoming the servant, steward, and lover of people the Lord requires you to be, the way to that place is His Word. Scriptures such as Provers 22:7, Acts 20:35, 1 Timothy 6:10, and Malachi 3:10 were anchor scriptures for me when looking to God to handle my finances. I trusted the process because it was rooted in Christ.

All these things revealed to me that it is a process to get where God wants me to be. The process has not been easy. I am still working on becoming that financially secure person the Lord wants me to be. But I have taken many necessary steps to get there, and I am striving closer to my goal each day. As you are becoming the person God ordained you to be, it will not be easy. There will be bumpy roads. You will deal with many obstacles. However, it is not wise to give up. It is all part of the process. And let us not grow weary while doing good, for in due season we shall reap if we do not lose heart. (Galatians 6:9 NKJV). You must continue to strive and become who God called you to be.

While watching an interview with Wes Morgan, the Lord spoke directly to me. While Wes' sister posed a scenario to him, that same scenario was posed to me by God. I can surely say I do not want God to reveal to me all the possible things I could have done for His kingdom but for me giving up or being too lazy to accomplish what God placed on my heart. We should all desire to hear, "Well done good and faithful servant." (Matthew 25:21 NKJV). Until you have heard those particular words from Jesus there is still fight in you. You still have room to better yourself. There is still work to do for the Kingdom. You are good, but you should continue to strive to be better. Even if you are one of the best in your area, it is wise to stay keen and current. You can also improve your craft in other areas. Kobe Bryant was one of my favorite athletes. Kobe did not give up after winning championships or breaking records. He continued to perfect his craft. His dedication and work ethic were what made him one of the best players to ever play the game of basketball. He made sacrifices to make time for what was important to him: his family and his career. You do not have to be a fan of his game to respect his grind. One thing we can all learn from the Mamba Mentality is to continue to press forward. Life will be full of wins and losses. We must learn lessons from them both to grow and strengthen who we are as individuals.

While you are becoming the best you through Christ, you must not compare yourself to those around you. You must become the best you. We sometimes look at what others have and desire to have it. We have no idea the price that came along with receiving it. We may see the glitz and glamour, but we do not see the struggle it took to get to that level or to keep it. Theodore Roosevelt said that comparison is the thief of joy. You cannot be content with the blessings you have before you if you are longing for what someone else has. You are unique. The "you" God has designed you to be is one of a kind. He has your very own special blessings awaiting you. You are a recipient of many blessings every day, yet you do not recognize them because you are too focused on what someone else has. Social media is a huge part of most of our lives. We see posts regarding "Goals" all the time. This could be relationship, body images, lifestyles, and the list goes on. However, we should all strive to be our own goal. That relationship could be on rocks behind closed doors. The body image could be altered or genetics. We are never sure if those huge houses are really homes to its occupants. And some of those $5,000 bags are filled with credit card debt. I do not know any of this with specificity. What I do know is people will only show you what they want you to see. The struggle is not regularly documented. Instead of coveting what your neighbor has, thank God for what you have and thanked Him in advance for the blessings to come. When I was going through my financial woes, I saw various people living what appeared to be their best lives on social media. I was genuinely happy for them especially those I knew who were truly happy. I was glad to see people able to afford lavish trips, cars, designer everything, and more. I knew what God had for me was for me. He was teaching me how to be a good steward of what I had. I was so thankful to be taught how to manage my funds, I refused to be envious of someone else doing good. My baby sister is a two-time homeowner, using one as rental property. I could not be prouder of her. My bestie is a credit repair guru and was changing the lives of people all over the world. I thanked God for blessing her and allowing her to be a blessing to others. Every time I saw someone around me being blessed, I thanked God. I knew He was in my neighborhood and my time was coming.

Pay careful attention to your own work, for then you will get the satisfaction of a job well done, and you will not need to compare yourself to anyone else. (Galatians 6:4 NLT). Whether it be in the office, the classroom, on social media, in recreational settings, never determine where you are in "becoming the best you" from where someone else is in "becoming the best them." The thing that separates us as followers of Christ from the world is that we know our reward is in heaven. Galatians 1:10 NIV states, "Am I now trying to win the approval of human beings, or of God? Or am I trying to please people? If I were still trying to please people, I would not be a servant of God. As a servant of God, we must be mindful that our treasures are in heaven. (Matthew 6:20). I think about the times I did care about what others said. I never outwardly showed it but hearing great things about me felt good. I do not think that is a bad thing. I do believe it can become a bad thing if you lean on and desire praise from others. While it is wonderful to know you are appreciated, never lose sight of the mission. The ultimate mission is to be a God pleaser. That is not always popular in our culture. Therefore, in some instances, you may have to decide between doing what is popular and what is right. Keep in mind these decisions are also part of your becoming.

Becoming a better you is specific to you. It is not doing what someone else is doing. And even if God gives you the vision to start a business that others already have, He will also make sure it is uniquely yours. Forever becoming for me meant to get my finances in order. I was so shocked when I reviewed my bank statements. I was spending $40 here, $12 there, and it was all adding up. I decided to budget better. I only spent what was in my budget to spend. Groceries, gas, bills, tithes, savings were all a must. It was not a must to get Starbucks, go out for happy hours, order wings. I had to learn to be financially responsible if I wanted to see real change. I wanted to become a better me with my finances, so I had to miss out on some things, I had to save and budget like crazy, but God never stopped providing. I had all my necessities and even some of my wants. God came through with an amazing position. I still do not remember even applying for the job. But I got a great job with a nice starting salary, benefits package, and I met one of my forever friends. It was all so divine. Once God saw I was doing right by Him and my finances in that position, more increase came. And He has been seeing me through non-stop.

This is not a sprint this is a marathon. It is continuous. God is always working on you and dealing with you in one area or another. At times He is dealing with you in multiple areas. Embrace the process. You will never "arrive" because there is always greater. However, the journey is the best part. Feel free to borrow my mantra as it was borrowed from another individual. Now that you have accepted that you are "forever becoming" and there are many opportunities to better yourself, trust God to lead you. He is the ultimate tour guide.

Ch. 10
Worth

I have said various times music does it for me. I love to be ushered into the Spirit. It is a feeling like no other when the words are exactly what are needed at the specific time. Like some of you, I was not always the most confident person. As humans we know we are not perfect, and we are lying to ourselves if we feel as if we are. No matter how pretty you are, there is someone prettier. No matter how shapely you are, there is someone even shapelier. There will always be someone better at a job or talent. That does not mean you are not worthy. Your worth is not in what you have or can offer, it is in Christ. Christ deemed you worthy when He died for you. (Ephesians 2:4-9; Romans 5:8).

Anthony Brown has a song simply titled "Worth." This song is one of the songs that made me understand my worth as a Christian and a woman of God. In the chorus he explains Jesus thinks we are worth saving. He thinks we are worth keeping. He thinks we are worth His death. In doing so, Jesus changes our lives, He cleans our insides, and He sacrificed His life so we could have everlasting life. It is more than a song. His Word expresses His love for us thoroughly. (Romans 8:35-39). I think about everything the Lord has done for me. God turned a premature crack cocaine addicted baby who was not given a chance at life by doctors into a mentor, an attorney, a wife, a God loving and God chasing woman. Nobody has done this much. If we are worth saving and keeping to God, we must really be something. Jesus Christ sacrificed His life. That is more than a big deal if I may say so myself.

I would not be honest if I said I always felt worthy. Not only did I not feel worthy of God's love, but I did also not feel like I was worth loving. My family loved me because they are family. Being good people, most of them showed me love. But there were always the ones I know disliked me for some reason I did not understand. Those who would smile in your face then say hateful things about you behind your back. Sometimes people are even bold enough to say certain things to you. Those people are so miserable with themselves they are trying to bring someone down to the bitter hole they feel stuck in.

Then of course after a failed relationship, broken heart, and several possible, but not possible, suiters, I did not know if I were worth love. It could be because you are single after having love encounters that never worked out, or single without having a special someone yet. There is a possibility you are in a relationship or marriage, and you are unhappy with that partner. But you do not feel like you deserve better. Sometimes you can be in relationship that you know deep in your heart this is not where you are supposed to spend forever for several reasons. This person does not know how to love you. This person cannot be trusted. This person does not have the same life values and desires. However, you contemplate if you deserve more than you are currently receiving. Being violated, not getting attention, loneliness, not being where you think you should be in life can all add to feelings of worthlessness.

However, these are all tricks of the enemy. The enemy wants you to feel like you are not good enough. He rather you think you cannot finish the book, lose the weight, get the degree, start the business, do the speaking engagement, or be successful in your own right. He does not want you to realize your potential. If you are not growing and glowing, Satan is happy. If you are not using the talents God showered on you, trust that Satan is rejoicing. If you have been stuck in dead-end jobs or dead-end relationships or at a dead-end in any aspect of your life,

Satan is hoping and wishing you stay right there. That allows the devil to win.

You must have the courage to come out that pit. Pits are not a fun place, but they can be so familiar that you stay there longer than necessary. A pit is described as a naturally formed or excavated hole or cavity in the ground; or a covered or concealed excavation in the ground, serving as a trap. Your pit can be a hole you dug yourself into or your pit can be a trap that was purposely construed for you to fall into. Either way, that is not your forever. Do not make that pit your home. The pit is not meant to be your permanent place. You are worth the palace; please never settle for the pit. My pit was temporary yet necessary for me to find a palace. Some pits are teaching lessons and your girl can be a professor after this one. Two jobs and studying for the bar while living with a friend, her two children, and occasionally the children's father was what I needed to find a suitable place to stay for my needs at the time and secure one job that could carry my financial load. I cannot express enough that getting out of this pit takes courage and confidence. The courage to escape the pit and the confidence to know you deserve the palace.

Courage is the mindset that enables a person to face difficulty with bravery. The words I purposely left out of this definition are *without fear*. By no means do I believe that you are fearlessly staying in the pit. Fear is what is paralyzing you. Real deal confidence comes when you are truly afraid, but you continue to follow God. I am tearing up right now because that has been my life so many times. I was afraid to apply to college. It had nothing to do with my ability. It had everything to do with rejection. I was not the biggest risk taker, so I only applied to two universities and was accepted to both. I was again afraid to apply to law school. I tried the same tactic and applied to only one school. I was devastated when I got the letter saying we regret to inform you.... I could not read the rest through my sobs. Once I got off the floor, bathroom floor to be exact, I took my heavy sobs to the shower and left them there. I came out that shower semi ready to face my fears. I was still beyond afraid of what the possibilities were and were not, but I would surely have a no if I did not try at all. I applied to numerous law schools including my own undergraduate university and either got waitlisted or denied. The pain hurt just as much each time. I was especially in my feelings with my own school waitlisting me. They probably wanted to say, "no mam Ms. wait to the very last minute to apply," so I decided I could not blame them for the waitlist. They were only an afterthought when I did not get into my number one school. Yet, I refused to give up. I got another letter from the original law school saying I may be eligible for a conditional program. If I pay a small fee, go to Michigan for a week to live in a hotel, and complete this law school bootcamp program of some sort, I could be admitted to law school as a part-time student.

I wish I could say I did all the things necessary and got on the first thing smoking from Tennessee to Michigan to demolish this bootcamp. That is not how it exactly went. Fear almost overtook me. I literally thought about everything in the world that could go wrong. What if I get lost driving nine hours alone? What if I am taken and my family has no idea how to retrieve me from my assailant? I knew they did not have that particular set of skills Liam Neeson had. What if I get there and everything is so hard, and I realize I am not attorney material? That was the real fear. My entire life my dream was to become an attorney. What if I was not attorney material? I am telling you all, the devil was busy. He had me thinking the absolute worst, and I was shaking in fear at this point. Thankfully, God was in control. I followed Him and paid the fee to do the program. I was accepted and had my itinerary. I was ready to beast bootcamp. Or was I? I seriously considered driving to my friends' apartment and hiding out there an entire week then telling my family, sorry they did not pick me although I did my best. I made the drive. Even on the drive I dreaded every moment. Nothing compared to me having to cross the Ohio River with my fear of bridges over water or gephyrophobia. It was no cake walk. The program was strenuous. I was a rookie to studying and was not sure of myself since this did not come with ease like before in college and high school. In the past, I could pay attention in class and take great notes; review my notes the night before an exam enough to memorize the information; and put everything I remembered on paper during the exam. That was an easy A or B only to forget everything right after the exam. However, every other no I got from those law schools was blind. Those schools had not met me. They did not make their decision based off my ability of actual legal reasoning and analysis. This time the bootcamp process I was partaking on was based off my own God given ability. I prayed every night. I said Lord, You have gotten me this far. Please continue to be with me. If this is for me, it's mine. If not, I know You have a greater path. I am trusting in You. To this day I am forever grateful for the conditional bootcamp program that led to my acceptance to law school and later my admittance to the Tennessee state bar.

The Bible says be strong and courageous, because you will lead these people to inherit the land I swore to their ancestors to give them. Be very strong and very courageous. (Joshua 1:6-7 NIV). It took courage. While I was terrified, I had to face the difficulties and face my fears. It took that courage for me to move forward in the next season God had for me.

I also had to be confident in myself as a child of God and more than anything, in God as my Lord to know I am palace material. I had to trust that God would do exactly what He said He would do. At that time, I knew I deserved more; however, I was not sure my more was a palace or for me, law school. Please believe me now when I say this, your more is a palace in whatever variation that is best fit for you. When you have confidence, you do not have to second guess if you are worthy of God's best. Second guessing yourself is how you stay in your pit that was only supposed to be temporary. Believe you deserve God's best because He said it. We all know the verse or some rendition of the verse where God speaks of the plan He has had for us and thoughts of peace to give us hope and a future. (Jeremiah 29:11). God made these plans before He formed us in our mothers' wombs. He wanted us to have the best before we knew who we were. He never changed His mind. There is no way a trap or hole in the ground is God's best. I refuse to believe that for myself, and I refuse to believe that for you. We are all worthy of so much more. You must truly believe it. Be confident in Him because His track record has not failed Him. All the promises God has made He never once let me down. I know I am no more special than any of you. I am willing to take a wild guess and say He never failed you either. Take your confident self and get out that pit. You are worth so much more because you are a royal priesthood. (1 Peter 2:9). Psalms says they confidently trust the Lord to care for them. (Psalms 112:7 NIV). Walk in that confidence all the way to your palace.

Please note, the enemy will still sneak back in. Once you are flourishing and truly walking in your purpose, he will be like a hawk. He wants to bring you back to that pit with him. There are different things that trigger those unworthy thoughts. Those thoughts will tamper with you periodically. Usually, it is something that we have forgotten about or tried to suppress purposely. It does not take much. It can be that one person who told you as a child that you would not be anything out of jealousy or spite.

Yet, that is something that sticks with you and makes you feel "less than" your entire life. A parent or guardian who did not know how to love you can cause those type of feelings. I am still needing more therapy sessions to talk about my mommy issues. These are all antics the devil is trying to use to make you stay in that low spot. If you realize how important you are to the Kingdom of God, you will succeed and continue to win souls over. Do not let the devil win this battle. Remember, this is not a battle of flesh and blood. (Ephesians 6:12) The devil wants your mind. Once he has your mind, he has control over you. Do not give him that opportunity. Use one of your most prayerful spiritual weapons: prayer.

We will not let the devil win. We will continue striving for God's best because we are courageous and confident. Even if you must put it on a post-it and place it somewhere you see it every day or verbally express it when you need your memory jogged. Never forget that you are courageous, confident, and worthy of God's best.

Ask God to reveal to you what made you get to that point of feeling unworthy. The Lord knows you, and He hears your prayers. Pour yourself out to Him in a way only you can. Ask God to take those feelings away. Pray to God just like you talk to your friends. It is a conversation. Allow Him to show you. God died for you while you were still a sinner; He truly loves you. (Romans 5:8). The Word says God covered you in your mother's womb and that you are fearfully and wonderfully made. (Psalms 139:13-14). Go to God with His Word. I know I had to do it and barely knew the Word. I was a work in progress. *Lord, You said I am Yours and You are mine. You said You would never leave me. Well, I sure feel alone. I need to know I am not. I need to know that You got me. Lord, I trust You but still I am human. Show me. I seriously need to know it is Me and you in this together on everything.* All I can say is I went to my God with His Word and was like okay God, do what You do. His Word shall not return to Him void. (Isaiah 55:11). You are important beloved. You are worth so much. If you are unsure what prayer to pray and mine above was not really your style, simply say: *God, I love You and I know You love me. I have been feeling this feeling of worthlessness and that I am less than. I know these feelings are not of You God. Reveal to me the source of these demonic feelings. I bind them now in Your son Jesus name. I bind every weapon against me. Remove these feelings immediately. I know I am an asset to You and Your Kingdom. I know my worth is in You and not in man. Lord thank You for loving me. Thank You for fighting this battle for me. I know You have already worked it out and I will rejoice now. I know I am worthy; I am courageous; I am confident. I am fearfully and wonderfully made. I am Yours and You are mine. In Jesus' name.*

I prayed many times to get over those little demons that tried to make me feel less than who God says I am. God filled me with His love, and I knew I had a purpose. I knew why He loved me. Far from perfect, He showed me my many flaws, some I did not want to admit. But I am free because He saved me. He saved me because He deemed me worthy. He deemed us all worthy because we are such. Praise God. I pray we all keep the courage to escape the pit, because multiple pits will come; and the confidence to know you deserve the palace each and every time life tries to tell you otherwise.

Anyone Can Get It

Thinking back on my days of having complete temper tantrums as a whole adult because I could not get my way is baffling. I can look back and laugh now, but no one was laughing who was on the receiving end of my foolery about the smallest things. Sadly, it was mostly about food. "You didn't think to order me food as well?" "What do you mean you don't want to go out to eat?" "So, are you saying you don't have the funds so my girls and I can go to happy hour?" Then it came to times when I was going through very stressful times, I was mean for no reason to those closest to me. I was not sure how to control my emotions to the point of dealing with the issue at hand. Instead, I would lash out and yell at the very person trying to help me. I have come a long way. I tell my husband Calvin he got the best version of me. He is probably shocked like wait this is the best. Ha! Remember I am forever becoming, but I can unequivocally say I am living my best most peaceful life not flipping out or going off on people. Every day is not going to be a highlight. Even with God, there will be low moments. Once you realize this, the easier it is to understand God is always with you. He is with you during the high moments and those low lonely moments.

I once heard someone say that if God is with you it means that things will be all good. I think that is always a misunderstanding of the Christian lifestyle. You see elders and leaders in the church appearing to be all put together and extremely happy. It does not appear that anything is going wrong in their lives. They could be in a season where things have all come together and they have little to no major issues. However, more likely than not, they are going through something as well. At one point, those same people were probably contemplating suicide, battling depression, popping pills, or drinking excessively just to get through the days. No one is without tribulations. John 16:33 reveals to us that in the world we will have tribulations. Because this world is not a perfect place, there will be ups and downs. Our journey will not be perfect not even as Christians because we are not perfect people. In the words of one of my friends, anyone can get it. When she gets angry it is time to get out the way because even innocent bystanders could possibly get the backlash of her attitude even though it is against someone else. She will forewarn you, that at that very moment anyone in her vicinity will feel her wrath. No one is exempt from troubles. No family is perfect. No marriage is without dispute.

Therefore, it is so important for us to be our true selves. I do not believe in over sharing. Better yet, let me say, I no longer believe in over sharing. I was once that person spilling out my guts on Twitter. I was telling the world of my 500 followers all my business. My account was private, and I never got over 500 followers. To this day, over a decade later, I still have less than 500 followers on my Twitter even though my account is now public. However, I learned that being my true self did not mean I had to tell every detail of my life to strangers, family, or friends. People were eating it up. I had no one to blame but myself. I was my own worst enemy by having word vomit on social media. I had no right to say anyone was in my business because I was openly sharing it all. At the time, I felt I was being real. "This is who I am," I said to myself. "This is what I am going through." "No one is going to tell my story like me." However, I was not using discernment in what to share.

I cannot thank God enough for discernment. We all have it. Some people call it the universe looking out for them, some people call it a woman's intuition. It is the inner guidance from your spiritual being. The more time you spend with God, the better your discernment. Common sense tells you not to go down the dark alley alone in a high crime area you are unfamiliar with when your cellphone is dead. Discernment tells you not to go for dinner and drinks with your girlfriends this time around although you have done it numerous times in the past. Sometimes it can be hard to explain to someone your decision when you have discerned this is not a good idea. That is even more reason to hold true to your convictions.

The Lord revealed to me that I was doing the most on Twitter. It did not take much. Simply spending more time with God, I spent less time on social media. When I started back posting regularly, I had no desire to post all my personal issues in a step-by-step 140-character manual. Trust me, I was still dealing with life's hassles. I began reflecting on my life differently. I stopped victimizing myself and started taking control. I started coming up with solutions so quickly, I had no reason to post my long-drawn-out problem. By no means was my life perfect. However, I was more selective with what I shared with others. I understood that everyone is not praying for you, many are out to prey on you. I had enough of being prey. I wanted to be part of my own healing and possibly help others in the process.

The helping others portion is when I realized so many Christians played perfect. So many of us were hesitant to show we had issues due to the fear of recoil or someone thinking you are far from God if you are dealing with turmoil. Some Christians are not necessarily afraid, but they know the power of praying and praising God through everything. Marvin Sapp has a song to Praise Him in Advance. Yes, I love it. Yes, I live it. I can praise my way through almost anything. I can be in my own pit feeling low as dirt. I praise God through it. Crying, shouting, thanking Him for simply being Him. It was helpful for me. It is helpful for almost any believer who tries it. It was not helping others. Remember I said it was about the helping others for me. Knowing that I was able to get through my storm or over my mountain meant nothing if I did not share it with someone else. Revelation 12:11 NIV says they triumphed over him by the blood of the Lamb and by the word of their testimony. It only helped me to have my testimony to myself. It only benefited me to know that God was my Provider and my Comforter through every trial and tribulation. Yet in order to lift up someone else, to show them God did for little ole me from South Memphis, Tennessee, I knew I had to tell my story to show that He would do it for others as well. I am a true believer that you do not go through your storm for yourself. You are a living testimony for others to see God through you.

Anybody can get it. Everybody will go through something. How I got through may not benefit everyone, but it can benefit someone. Being vocal is the only way to show that it is possible. I know some good Christians may not agree with me in this one. I learned this one and will never go back on. Therapy is a healing process. Do not rebuke me. Yes, I believe in God and therapy. I believe God gave us therapist just as he gave us doctors and teachers. Therapy is a key to doors we have closed shut in order not to feel. Yet feeling and being vulnerable is the only way to heal. I know vulnerability is scary. You are fully exposed to any and everything when you let your guard down. In this place of vulnerability, you will heal. Please do not take this as me saying go wear your heart on your sleeve. Remember, we are doing all these things with discernment. God is not telling any of us to be vulnerable to someone we just met from swiping right and now we have no idea why they are leaving us on read. That is not what I am saying either. You must be in a safe place which is different for everyone. For me, that place was on the couch in front of my therapist.

From The Crushing to The Crown

Therapy taught me that I could live without dependency on others. Therapy taught me that man's love is no comparison to the love of Jesus Christ. You may have learned that at age 11. You may have never needed to sit on a couch to catch that revelation. But for the person still dealing with codependency or searching for love in the wrong places, my method of praising God through it all may not be enough. You are possibly dealing with layers and years of depth of whatever you are going through. If no one ever shares their story of therapy, that person could still be struggling. To help someone else, I refuse to play perfect. To help someone else, I tell my business with discernment. I can promise you the Lord has urged me to share more than my liking. I say, "Lord, I know you have someone else to share that one. Do people need to know I went through that too?" When you hear the voice of the Lord asking, "Whom shall I send, who will go for Us, do you want to say not me God or do you want to say Here am I. Send me." (Isaiah 6:8).

In my flesh, I was thinking Jesus stop playing. You are going to have to send someone else, anyone else, because people do not need to know me on that level. Praise God I allowed God to use me. Being honest about your dismay and mishaps as a follower of Christ is your, "Here am I. Send me!" I promise you the leader of the praise team, the usher who smiles with open arms, the pastor him or herself, has issues. God never told us we would be without tribulation. What He did say is to be of good cheer because He has overcome the world. (John 16:33). Do not miss your shout. No worries, I can shout enough for the both of us. He already overcame every obstacle we face. There is nothing too hard for our God. He has us covered. I refuse to move as if I did this alone. I refuse to move as if God did not get me through at my lows and hold me up in my highs. Because He has been my all, I know I have a responsibility to share it with others. Yet, another reason I am so thankful to see those with a huge platform being vulnerable. The Erica Campbells and the Kirk Franklins have posted on their social media requesting prayer. It shows how human they are and that no matter how "big" you get that you are not alone. We are a family in this thing together.

I was texting a friend who is a non-believer. He used to believe but had questions. Now he simply chooses not to believe. He was a huge gamer and annoyed me like no other. I asked if I had an annoying trait he could remember. He reminded me of the social media posting. I literally laughed out loud and told him people were eating it up until all my posts were about God. He then said, "Well that is because they have the Bible." While that is facts, most people will not read the Bible. I know people who will delete the Bible app from their phone as soon as space is needed. The Bible is often used as a bedtime remedy when you are having a hard time to go to sleep. I know this one firsthand. If I am the only Bible or follower of Christ people see, I want to be my authentic self. I want to show that while I know God is real and with me, I still have struggles. God shows Himself in every struggle. I lean on God not because I was told to do so, it is because I know where my help comes from. (Psalms 121).

Jesus Himself was crucified by the very people who cried out Hosanna a week prior. It did not take but a mere three days for our King to rise. (Matthew 21; Mark 15-16). It feels good to know that I do not go through these times without my heavenly Father. As I stated, anyone can get it. Anyone can also have God. The love of God is free for all. Since we know that, no matter the circumstances, we will have trials, who better yet to have go through these trials with you other than the One who has overcome them all?

If you are of the mentality that anybody can get these hands, anybody can get cursed out, think about it. Anybody can get delivered, anybody can get an intimate relationship with Christ. While any and everybody still will have issues, God got you. And who better would you want to get life with, when those obstacles do come.

Make a [Good] Day of It

𝓘 have always loved school. No matter what, I wanted to go to school. The only time I struggled getting up for school was when I was sick. Yet, I would still make myself get out of bed. Well, I am also an asthmatic, and it was extremely severe as a child. One day I woke up and I could barely breathe. I did not want to tell my mom. I knew she would make me stay home, or worse take me to the hospital. Being left in my hospital bed for hours from what was supposed to be a smoke break by my mom was not anything I looked forward to. I knew that was not the move for me. This day, I played it off as if I were okay. I was short of breath just getting dressed for school. I was determined to go to school. In class my teacher asked me to take the attendance roll to the office. Any other day this would have been pure excitement. I was the teacher's pet and did all the little errands. But I thought about those stairs, and I instantly felt suffocated. Well, I could not say I was sick. So, I took the roll down. It took me double the time, and I wanted to just lay out in the hall. I took multiple breaks and got water. I made it through that day. The next day I was sick, but not as bad as the day before. I went at it and did my best. The third day I was only a little sick. I could take almost a complete deep breath without wheezing. On the fourth day I was back at one hundred percent. No one ever knew I was sick all those days. Now that I think about it, it was probably not the best that my mom and stepdad or even my siblings went three full days without knowing anything was wrong with me. That issue is for another day.

Similarly, we do not see the trials other Christians are enduring. They put a smile on because they have faith God has already worked it out. It is not fake; it is walking and talking believing that God is doing or will do what He said He would do. In my case, it was Him as a Healer. He did just that for me. Remember while some people are at their day four, others are still in day one, two, or three. Either they are at day four of one hundred percent, or they are patiently waiting on that season to arrive. Allow everyone to have their day; show grace in the process.

It is easy for me to say, "Get at His feet and pray. Give it all to Him." Most of us know this. We know to get in His presence when we want to feel Him. It does not mean it will stop you from having a low day. A day you were not feeling your best, looking your best, thinking your best. You could be off your A game. Do not take that as God not being with you. He is still there. He is allowing you to develop in the process. Think about what you are allowing to control your mind that got you to this point. Whatever controls your mind and thoughts control you. (Proverbs 23:7).

If you are constantly worried about how bills are going to get paid, that may make for a bad day. When I was going through my financial woes, even knowing I could easily make a call or two to get what I needed, I was not having the best of days. If your feelings are hurt by something your boo did or said, it will have a tremendously negative impact on your day. Calvin tells me if he is upset with me his workday is trash because that is literally all he thinks about that day. Maybe you are in mourning, you have been working too hard, you cannot find a job to later complain about how hard you work. If any of these things or something similar is taking over your mind that could cause a bad day. Do not allow your day to be bad. Use different outlets to overcome the enemy.

Write, paint, draw, workout, sing or play uplifting songs, listen to motivational music, talk to someone you can confide in, talk to God, exercise self-care. These are just a few things you can do to lift your spirits. When I wake up and realize my attitude or mood is messed up, I know my day is already off to a bad start. I make the conscious decision to thank God for all He has done, is doing, and is going to do. I thank Him for the opportunity to make Him proud again and another chance to get it right. As strange as it sounds, I also instantly begin talking to myself.

Of course, I talk to myself. We are all guilty of it. We may not all respond back and sometimes the conversation is in our heads only, but it is still there. As I brush my teeth for the two to three minutes that is suggested every morning, I look at myself in the mirror and thank God. I thank Him for the smallest thing, like having a toothbrush and toothpaste. I thank Him for major things like the roof over my head and the safe living space. I tell myself since God woke me up, it is purpose in my day. I will not allow myself or anyone else to get in the way of God's purpose for my day. It is a lot that can be said while brushing your teeth. I forgot to mention that I do this on my toes. I have small calves and I was told that standing on my tiptoes can strengthen my calves and eventually grow them. So, I have teeth-brushing pep talks on my tiptoes daily. My balance is sometimes off, but the mission is clean teeth and motivation. I am usually good at meeting those goals.

There are questions that could be good to ask you or ask God even. *Am I too consumed with myself? Why am I in my feelings? Am I mad at [insert name here] and for what? What did I do to add to the problem? What can I do to make it better? Does this glorify God? Does this edify me, or others involved? Could it be worse? Am I outside the will of God? What does God want me to get out of this? Should I focus on this? Is this a battle for God? Is this even my business? Is there a current solution I can aid in?* This is not a complete list. The questions are endless. You know what to ask yourself in the process. Do not just ask but get the answers. You will not be at peace until you know the root of these unhealthy feelings. While the feelings are unhealthy know that they are human. You are not any less of a person or a Christian because you are feeling down some days. God uses these moments to draw closer to you. Do not allow these moments to pull you away from Him. Overcome them. You will be glad you did.

One thing that people say is, "Today is just not my day." That is false. Jesus woke you up; today is your day. He has a reason for opening your eyes and breathing breath into your body every day you are alive. Never think that it is not your day. Your days will not be the same. But it is truly a day God has made, rejoice in another opportunity to get it right and honor Him. (Psalm 118:24). And if you truly feel like this day is going to be a bad day or it has been a bad day, challenge yourself to end it on a high note or to make tomorrow even better.

Remember early when I spoke about my morning pep talk over my morning teeth-brushing session on my toes? Well, I do something similar at night. I brush my teeth before bed, on my tiptoes again. My calves have not shown much progress at all. I should probably stop, but I feel like if I stop will be right before I see major growth and will have to start from scratch all over again. But the conversation in my mirror is a normal one. If I am feeling sluggish as if the day defeated me, I give it over to God. I said Lord, I was not up to working out how I should. I had this feeling of defeat that got in the way of me moving in excellence the entire day. I know I can do better, and I will be better. Lord, you got me through this day. I know we are all dealing with something, but the best of me did not show up today. I pray I get the opportunity to make you proud tomorrow.

This is not me feeling sorry for myself. This is me recognizing that some days are more difficult than others. Around my father's birthday and Father's Day and even some major holidays, I am on the struggle bus. I am listening to David Ruffin one moment and Jeezy the next moment. I want to feel that feeling I felt when I had my father with me so I would listen to the music he played when we would ride together. Yes, I love God. Yes, I worship and praise God. Yes, I know with my whole heart that God loves me. Yet, I still have difficulties. I still get emotional. I still have mood swings. I still miss those I love that are no longer here for me to tell them. I take things out on Calvin when he is only showing that he is caring and concerned. We are not exempt from having personal issues because we follow God.

If you do not tell people or social media what you are dealing with, no one will know. It is the same way for that seasoned saint you see weekly all put together. They may have had to take a personal day from work to get away from reality. They could be suffering from a serious illness and believing God for complete healing. We do not know. Instead of making the day about you, try to make someone else's day better. Pay a compliment to someone. That does not cost a thing. When you make eye contact with someone smile and nod. That is usually how we southerners speak to complete strangers. Do not be creepy or weird with it. And if you are located somewhere where smiling at strangers is not socially accepted, find an alternative that still shows the God in you.

Remember that the day is what you make it. And sometimes you simply are not up to making it excellent but know that God saw purpose in having you in it. Give yourself grace as well. While showing grace to others, know that you deserve that same grace. Every day may not be perfect, but every day is worth it. Or whatever Kirk Franklin said.

Ch. 13
Give up on God... Then what?

Every Christian, who is truly walking, has had some hard times. That comes with the territory. No one will be without trials and tribulations. Sometimes we feel like people are better off without being fully committed to Christ. You see people on the fence or off the fence completely prospering. It is disheartening when you are in the desert. A little voice creeps up telling you that you are better off giving up on God as well. But are you really?

I have a friend Kelsey who is such an amazing spirit. She is a giver, a planner, a hard worker, and an overall great person. Sometimes when Kelsey is overwhelmed by everything that is happening in her life she goes into seclusion. It helps her to get closer to God. I texted her during one of her withdrawals from everyone and she said, "Princess I sometimes just want to give up on God. Look at all this I am dealing with day in and day out. I am faithful, but I want to give up."

I felt Kelsey's pain through that very text message. I had once been there myself. I knew what it felt like to think you were better off not being all in. People everywhere were "prospering", and they were not faith walkers. I came to a point where I asked myself if I give up on God what are my other options. I was instantly afraid.

I knew giving up on my Jesus meant I was removing myself from His covering, and that is a scary thought. I knew it meant not being able to lay at His feet when I wanted to be in His presence and feel the Holy Spirit comfort me. I knew it meant going out on a limb making major and small decisions without God's wisdom. I knew it meant not rejoicing every morning for another day and being thankful every night for making it through the day. I knew it meant not being able to cry out to Him whenever I needed Him. I knew it meant not always having His grace with me. I knew it meant my inability to pray to Him various times of the day and enjoy our conversations. I realized it meant losing my Best Friend, my Father, my Provider, my Comforter, my Shoulder, my Everything. So yes, I was very afraid of quitting on Jesus.

While I was afraid, I understood where Kelsey was coming from. I did not have to be going through the same thing to empathize with her. It was a feeling almost every Christian has felt before or will feel at some point. Doing all you can do and still feel like it's not enough. Being faithful and still not getting out of your own pits. I learned the doing and the being meant nothing. God was not moved by our being good or doing good. He wants our hearts. And when He truly has our hearts, we are not trying to leave Him at every bad turn. I think about how hard I fought in relationships to make things work. Even with the signs, I was willing to still work on us. I wanted it so much. I would say well let's figure out the disconnect. Let's think of a master plan. Maybe we should spend more time together. Maybe we should be intentional about our time together. That is how it should be with God. When things go left our first, second, or even third thought should not be to get out. It should be to work on the relationship. The relationship with Christ is what sustains us. It does not matter how much good you do or how good you are being, strengthening the relationship is key.

Weighing the pros and cons, giving up on God was not as glamorous as I thought it would be. Then the Lord dropped a few things in my spirit. I will share those with you all in hopes that it can be just as helpful as it was for me.

1. Those people who are outside His will that appear to be prospering are broken and empty.

Some of the men are driving lavish cars, with physically beautiful women, hustling legally or illegally, and making a nice amount of money. Yet these men are not whole. They look to material things or women to justify them. They have not allowed Christ in or have walked away from Christ because His way did not consist of the fame and glamour they wanted for their own lives.

The women are married, mothers, successful jobs or stay at home moms. But that marriage is empty. She is his trophy he shows off and only loves for self-glorification. She was not ready for those children and caring from them and her husband has called unbearable stress. She shops to fill the voids, but it does not get the job done.

These people smile on the outside, show off their fancy lifestyle, then go home and cry themselves to sleep at night. They have no peace. They decided to leave God in the background because His will did not end with the success story they wanted it to be. Their paths did not line up with the paths God had for them, and it meant more to them to do their own thing. They gave up on God and gained "stuff" but lost peace, joy, and love.

2. I have given up on Him many times.

During these times I did not realize my actions were showing I had given up on God. While I still thought about God, I was not letting Him in my life how He should have been. I lacked faith. And not to the point of, "I believe but help my unbelief." I had no belief. I had allowed the world to make me believe the ways of God were not possible for me. There were times I did not believe anything was possible. The word says if you believe that a mountain can be moved, you have the power to move it. (Matthew 17:20). That mountain is anything huge you are dealing with at the time. I thought that was a joke. I felt what was done was done and my thoughts and beliefs that things would change wouldn't change it. I was so wrong.

I did not fully trust God to lead me. I gave Him what I thought He should have, not everything. When you fully trust God, you allow Him total control over the largest, the smallest, and everything in between. It was easy for me to say I trusted God when everything around me was going smoothly. Soon as I got some rocks on my nice gravel I felt fear, anxiety, and worry. When you trust God, those things will be a thing of the past. Yes, you will get scared, anxious, concerned, stressed, but you will know to hand it all over to God. Lay it in His hands and let Him deal with the issue. You will be glad you did.

Without verbalizing it, I walked away when I started spending less and less time with Him. I gave other things and people the time I should had given Him, in turn, making them my god. That thing varied from my boyfriend to my nieces and nephews to my own plan for my life. God is a jealous God. He wants no god before Him. (Exodus 34:1). This does not mean you are building golden statutes or worshipping the sun, moon, and stars. It is glorifying that Instagram model too much. Praising that couple because they show you all their highs and a select few lows, so you know they are still human. Where your treasure is, is where your heart is also. (Luke 12:34). If your heart is with God, He is your treasure. He is your prize possession. However, if your heart is with bae, work, status, fame, material things, those things are your treasure. Freely give God His time. He is your God and Savior; He does not deserve anything less.

3. I gave Satan too much credit.

Things were happening in my life I could not explain. Well, let me be completely honest. Some things I could explain because I knew better when I first got myself in those toxic situations. I had full control, yet I used my free will for bad. I live with those choices. Remember, you cannot blame God for harsh consequences after you knew you were doing wrong in the first place. Let's be thankful for grace and mercy knowing that the wages of sin is death. (Romans 6:23). When you know that the act you are participating in is wrong, you feel it. Sometimes it can feel like an outer body experience or actions in slow motion while giving you a mental moment of clarity. Conviction is what I call this. It's wrong, you know it's wrong, you even feel bad about the wrong. Still, you carry on as if there is no reason to stop. Be mindful of these things by thinking first.

Other times I kept getting demonic attacks out the blue. I would say, "The devil is really busy." I was not realizing that God was allowing Satan to move to save me from myself. I was getting ready to dig myself deeper and deeper into the pit. Jesus knew that He had to hurt me, take something from me, remove some stuff, give me something I couldn't handle on my own, and right out drop me to my knees.

These things made me draw closer to God. I realized I needed Him more than I had ever admitted. It was time to stop getting mad at Satan for the drama, take responsibility for my own mess, and start thanking God for the drastic changes that drew me closer to Him.

4. He never once stopped loving me.

After all the things we do God still loves us. Jesus loved us enough to die for us when we were still sinners. (Romans 5:8). I pondered giving up on God. We do not say this because we feel He has given up on us. If we are honest with ourselves, even in the storm we have a lingering feeling that He is still there.

I broke His heart. I bared the name "Christian" while doing ungodly things. I was a mess. He forgave me. He never left me. I was far from perfect. I was mean sometimes for no reason at all. I wished bad things on people. I wanted my way all the time. I think I was obsessed with getting my way. Those were my personal wins. God never said, "Well this one here is just too crazy I have done all I can for her. I am going to leave her be." Instead, He said, "This is my child. I know she does not realize what she is doing. I love her. I will stay with her through it all and keep her covered because I have a plan to prosper her. (Jeremiah 29:11). Yes, I have to allow her some heartache and hard times, but I will not force her back into my arms. I will not allow her death because her work here is not done. I will never stop showing her my love even when she does not want to receive it."

And Jesus feels the same way about you. He allowed me to make these decisions on my own. He is allowing you to live your life. He gave us free will; He will never take it away. We have the ultimate choice if we want to use the free will God gave us to be in His will or out of it.

***

The next time things get rough, because there will always be a next time, ask yourself this: are you willing to give up on God or get closer to God?

We were created in His image. (Genesis 1:27). We are His righteousness. (2 Corinthians 5:21). He sees us without blemish or wrinkle. (Colossians 1:22). If we make the decision to give up on God, we are ultimately making the decision to give up on ourselves. There is no eternal life without God and the only way to get to God is through His Son Jesus. (John 14:6). You do not even have to ask yourself what's next once you give up on God. If it is not spending eternity with Him, the other option is not considerable. Lean into God how you can receive it before allowing yourself to think He is no longer an option to be considered at all.

The Lord Gives and the Lord Takes Away (Or does He?)

We rave about how good God is. All the time, God is good. And God is good, all the time. It's a thing believers say. One believer to another, we know how to start it and finish it. For some reason, it is so rare for us to speak openly about God's no's or what He took from us. Nobody wants to hear God gave me something to love, to cherish, to adore, only to hear then He took it away. It does not matter if these things are designer clothes, expensive cars, talents, amazing careers, finances, a sound mind, or loved ones. The last thing you want is that "taketh away" portion we have all heard about growing up.

Truth be told, my life has consisted of "taketh away" after "taketh away." I did not know how to handle this. I remember one day when God had vividly told me this man I "knew" was supposed to be my husband was not the man He had for me. At this point I am feeling Eli is a thing of the past. Sly comes in and is taller, smarter, and just as attractive. I kept thinking well Eli was not it because Sly is. False. I was so angry. I wanted to give God a good clapping my hand with every word speech about how He had me messed up and how I was not the one or the two. I stayed ready for a good debate, and this was no different. Who was I kidding? This was Jesus. My Savior. As livid as I was, I went to God the best way for me. I journaled. That day I let it all out with my pen on how God continuously took everything from me. I said *that's fine God. Clearly all You want me to have is You. You want me to be completely Yours and to share me with no one else. Every time I love someone You say no and take him away. So, I hope You're happy. I am all Yours and only Yours. You are the only person who has me. So be ready for me to be consumed with nothing but you and vice versa. It's just me and You. Period.*

I know many of you may wonder how I was bold enough to say something like that to God. Why I would even feel the need to express myself in that manner to Him. It was because I was tired of God taking things from me. Duh, it was simple. I said before that getting my way was personal little victories. So, in these instances I was losing. And I was not happy about that. He was working on me. Whew I thank You for deliverance even now, Lord. My plan consisted of me being with Sly. My plan was to be married to him and eventually have his babies. My plan was to be the modern-day Cosby family. Did I mention he was working on his doctorate? Of course, we all know God laughs at our plans. God said He knows the plan He has for you. (Jeremiah 29:11a NIV). God has already made a divine plan for our lives. And His plan consists of peace and hope. (Jeremiah 29: 11b NKJV). It does not matter what we have planned to do. If it is not ordained by God, it is nothing. Although at the time I felt I was supposed to marry Sly, God knew he was not the best for me. He also knew that I would continue down a very destructive road if He did not snatch from me what I thought I wanted. That is a shouting moment. God sometimes has to derail our plans for us to stay on course with what He has in store.

Once I recovered emotionally, it took me a minute, I stayed even closer to God. After all, He wanted me solely for Himself anyway. You are getting all of me, Jesus. God begin to drop different nuggets in my spirit about Sly. Things became extremely clear as to why he was not who I was supposed to be with. If I had continued down that road, I would have been miserably unhappy. God was saving me from my own way, and I had no idea. 1 Peter 1:5-7 explains how God's power keeps us and shields us. At times you may not realize God is covering you, or you may want what you want so badly you are willing to sacrifice God's covering for a moment of happiness. Instant gratification is hazardous. I would have eventually lost the person I was, my true self, trying to become the person Sly wanted me to be instead of the person God knew I could be. Still, God is continuously keeping watch over us. He has given me no's on moving, no's on jobs, no's on going off on people who were completely wrong. I started to get excited about these no's once I realized God loved little ole me enough to ensure I do not drive myself in the wrong direction. God was the captain of my ship, and I was blessed to have Him as my anchor. Keep your faith. If God told you something, everything He is removing in the process is preparing you for the promise. If you received what felt like a million no's and God taking away everything you wanted, start getting excited because that promise is even closer to your doorstep.

I did not realize it at the time, but Jesus saved my life when He blocked that relationship. The most important things in a Christ-like relationship were lacking in this one. Things such as a prayer life where you can pray together and pray for each other, real love, true friendship, and vulnerability were all missing. Yes, I was open to all those things, but I learned Sly was not. No matter how much he was into my intellect, my body, my personality, he was not willing to share some of the most important things. Praying together and for each other, complete vulnerability, are necessary to me. But for God taking that relationship away from me, I would have been in a relationship that I would have emotionally died in. Sly wanted us to have our own separate relationships with God. I was so gone I even start thinking well maybe I should be happy he has a personal relationship with God. Only God knew where He was taking me. Because of that God also knew that Sly was not the man for where I was going.

Saying that I would have been miserable is an understatement.

Think back on the times God told you that person you were so head over heels about was not His best. How did you react? Did you ever ask God to make that person the one although He had revealed this was not for you? Have you ever been so upset with God you said or thought some things you wish had never been said or thought? Did you defy God and end up brokenhearted? Did you defy God and end up in a relationship with no growth?

Like some of you, my answer to almost every question was yes. Then I thought to myself, *only if I had let that thing go when God first revealed those factors to me. I would not have wasted so much time. I would not have caused so much pain.* If you have already come to a point where God said no, just let go in peace. You save yourself some trouble if you completely surrender to the plan God has for your life. Jesus loves you more than you will ever know. He wants the absolute best for you. If He has revealed to you this thing you are so attached to is not of Him, it must go. Matthew 6:33 tells you to seek the Kingdom of God and His righteousness first, and all things will be added to you. Anytime you are willing to put something else before God, not only are you doing yourself a disservice, but you are hurting God. I do not know about you, but I am tired of breaking God's heart.

Maybe you are saying you have already been there, and you are dealing with the aftermath of getting that thing taken away from you. A lot of us have been there. You are not alone by any means. Know that with each day you will get stronger. The word of God is your best friend. David went through a time where he felt he was all alone because his people wanted to kill him. David even felt that God had forgotten about him. (Psalm 13:1). He was literally fighting for his life, but he kept his faith in God. In 1 Samuel 30:6, David stayed focus on God which led to his strength. Nothing is wrong with being emotional over that thing you wanted. But know if God took that from you, He has something much better in store. Reminds me of the social media image. Although it is a poor portrayal of Jesus, I understand the lesson. Jesus is asking the little girl to hand Him the teddy bear she loves so dearly while holding a bigger, better teddy bear behind His back that she cannot see. You may not see a glimpse of it now, but trust and believe what God has for you is truly for you. That college He wants for you, the career He wants for you, the family He wants for you, the life He wants for you, these things are all obtainable. However, if you never put the past in the past, you cannot enjoy the present, and may miss out on what God has planned for your future. Allow Him to take away your current knowing that it will be replaced with His best.

I started this chapter off by saying God has taken what He gave me many times. I have lost a grandmother, a nephew, friends, and other family members. Nothing could have prepared me for the loss of my father. It literally hurts to my core to even type out these words. Losing my father was the most difficult period in my life. I will never forget the day, the pain, the hurt, the anger, the fear, the confusion, the emptiness, the lack of control, and how small and insignificant in this world I felt. Wednesday, December 23, 2015, I was headed home to Memphis. My dear friend rode with me for the first time ever having a riding buddy, but I was happy not to be alone. We got on the road later than expected, but riding with a partner, talking, singing, catching up, always made for good times. Driving to my daddy and the rest of my family for the Christmas holiday, I got a call that literally made my heart skip a beat. He's gone. My daddy had been shot down on the porch of someone he deemed a friend. He was taken from me. A calculated murder for hire. My head is pounding all over again thinking about it. That is when my life changed forever. I felt empty. I felt unsafe, uncovered. Very much like David, I was a wreck emotionally and could not deal with the pain. My goal was to continue allowing God to have my whole heart. While my father had an unclean past, he was the greatest father a girl could ask for. God surely gave exceedingly abundantly when He gave me my father. Of course, that is why it was so hard for me to come to terms with losing this great man, my king. It was not from a long-time illness, Covid-19, or a crash. He was taken from me, and I will forever feel robbed of my mind and my earthly protector and best friend. While my heart was devoted to Jesus, as a human, I was at my lowest.

I was confused. I was hurting. I was angry. I was without the only man who I know without a doubt that he loved me completely, and I had his heart. Do you understand that kind of love? Have you ever encountered love so amazing? If you have not, please accept the love of God right now. God showed you that kind of love when He sent His only Son to die for you on Calvary. (John 3:16). God shows you that kind of love when you are not punished for every sin we commit. (Romans 6:23). God shows you that kind of love when He allows you to prosper despite your shortcomings. (Lamentations 3:22). The entire reason you can love is because God loved you first. (1 John 4:19).

I was so focused on what God had taken away from me I was unable to see what He had given me. So many people around me had horror stories when it came to their fathers. Yet, I was blessed with an amazing daddy. I made the mistake of looking at how little time I had with him instead of looking at how much time I got to enjoy with him. Some people around me still have fathers alive and they have yet to experience moments like the ones I shared with my father. Was I devastated? Yes. Does it still hurt? As I hold back tears, absolutely, yes. However, the times we shared together are some of the best memories I have in my life. I would not trade our laughs, our cries, and our relationship for anything in this world. Instead of looking at your greatest losses as "why me moments" take the time out the thank God for what He did give you. If you only had your parents for a short amount of time, be thankful. If you are troubled by your family, thank God for your friends or coworkers who keep you sane. And if you downright feel like it is you and only you, be thankful that God deems you so special He wants you to Himself a little while longer.

One of the most important things I learned from my father's murder is that God is everlasting. At the time, I could not grasp that God felt He needed my daddy more than I needed him. Clearly, I was still in need of a father. God showed me it was more about Him needing me more. At no point should anything come before God. There is no person, place, or thing that could love you more than Christ. Everything I thought I was missing was everything God always had right there in front of me. Now, time spent allowing the Holy Spirit to completely run free in my life has been the best time ever.

In losing my beloved father, I learned to love my Heavenly Father even more. I learned to trust God with my whole heart. I learned to lean and depend only on God. While I said I was doing all those things beforehand, my daddy was my "go to" for most things. I learned that I must go to my Heavenly Father first about every situation; God should never play second to anyone or anything in your life. While my dad had a solution to almost everything, it was not guaranteed. My God has a solution to everything, and He has a one hundred percent track record.

God taught me what it meant for Him to be a Father to the fatherless. (Psalm 68:5). If you are dealing with the pain of losing a parent or loved one, I will not give you the cliché saying, "God makes no mistakes." While that is true, no one wants to hear that when they are hurting. I know I didn't. I find myself randomly thinking about fun times about with my daddy and I will all over again ask God are you sure You got this right because he was my guy, my big homie. I will say, God's decisions consider your entire life and your eternity. We think in the moment rather it be short term or long term. The timeframes do not compare to. God thinks eternity. His plans have your future in mind. (Jeremiah 29:11). You should trust only God to make decisions for your eternity.

In the healing process, continue to lean on God. God will take some things away. However, God is strengthening you. That pain you never thought you would get over is becoming more bearable each day. Continue giving it to God. Remember, everything we have God has given it to us, we are mere stewards. God comes back for what He allows us to have for the time being, He will be back for you as well.

Taste and See that the Lord is Good

*H*ave you ever had your mouth watering for the perfect meal? Something so savory, so deliciously appetizing, you could not wait until you were able to peacefully enjoy that very meal. That meal for me is perfectly seasoned wild caught salmon, cooked long enough that it has a crisp top but not too long that it is still juicy and flavorful; homemade smoked gouda mac n cheese, collard greens slowly cooked with smoked turkey, an array of seasoning, and a hint of vinegar; sliced candy yams cooked in a cast iron skillet coated with butter, sugar, and vanilla until tender; and homemade buttermilk cornbread. This meal is heaven to me. At any time, the salmon can be interchanged with a medium cooked ribeye tossed in garlic butter. Food is life and now I am ready to get in this kitchen. That amazing lip licking delicious meal is one that you simply must experience for yourself to get the full understanding of how it stops you in your tracks. That is exactly how it is when you try Jesus. Jesus is the best thing that ever happened to me and everyone else who genuinely gave Him a try.

The word says to taste and see that the Lord is good. (Psalm 34:8). This is not a literal tasting like that appetizing meal you could not wait to have. It is even better than that. This is the everlasting taste of Jesus Christ in your mind, body, and soul. It is a feeling of fullness and completeness that cannot be found anywhere else. It cannot be duplicated in any other way. There are times you may not feel whole. Instead of latching on to a new job, a new craft, a new bae, trying to feel whole, latch on to God. Only the fullness of God can make you whole. In John 6:35 Jesus declares "I am the bread of life. Whoever comes to me will never go hungry, and whoever believes in me will never be thirsty. That feeling, that desire you have for more comes from God. When you are ready to fully receive everything He has for your life, you accept Jesus Christ as your Lord and Savior. Jesus will feed your spirit. He will ensure you are spiritually full of His Word. After all, in the beginning was the Word, and the Word was with God, and the Word was God. (John 1:1) When your spirit is full of God's Word you will never go hungry. The Word will always be with you, leading you, teaching you. When your spirit is full of God's word you will not thirst. You will no longer have to have voids filled because Jesus would have already filled every void. The more you allow the Holy Spirit to fill you up through prayer, meditation, reading the bible, fasting, and applying what God reveals to you daily, you will have a full life.

Maybe it is only me, but I get to a point even when I am hungry that I can name everything I do not want to eat but I have a hard time pinpointing exactly what it is I have a taste for. I think we have all been at that point. I get that feeling when I feel like I have eaten so many different things lately but having any of those things will not be satisfying to my current appetite. Well, my friends, when you have tried many things, many distractions, many outlets, and nothing has worked, I promise you when you try Jesus you will be reasonably satisfied. Take the woman with the issue of blood. She had this issue for twelve years. She had spent all her money going to all the specialists about her issue. Still, she was still dealing with her problem and had been getting worse instead of better. She had become an outcast in the community because she was seen as unclean. She still had faith that merely touching Jesus could make her whole. She mustered up everything she had in her, no matter how unclean she appeared to be, she made her way through that crowd and touched Jesus and was immediately healed. Jesus told the woman that her faith healed her and that she could go in peace, suffering no more. (Mark 5:25-34).

All it takes is a little bit of faith to try Jesus. And the miracles He will do in your life are indescribable. Think how bad off the woman with the issue of blood could have been had she not tried Jesus. She had already suffered for twelve years. What other turmoil would she have had to encounter without Jesus? Something as simple as reaching out and pressing up against Jesus, can turn your world from chaos to peace. If you must press through the crowds, the noise, the partying, the failed relationships, the dysfunctional family, the hunger pains from the empty fridge simply to get to Jesus, do what needs to be done. You will be glad you did.

Trying Jesus does not mean life will suddenly become perfect. There will always be someone or something trying to block you from your blessing. The closer you get to God, the more upset the devil gets. Be mindful of the ones who happily listen to your problems but find something better to do when you want to converse about your joy. Jesus said, "You will be hated by everyone because of [M]e, but the one who stands firm to the end will be saved." (Matthew 10:22 NIV). People may dislike you even more because of the God in you; it has nothing to do with you personally. However, Jesus will give you the tools needed to get through any situation. God never said that you will never be tempted. He also never said that it would be easy. His Word says God will give you a way out and a way of escape. (1 Corinthians 10:13). When you are rooted in Christ and acknowledged how good He is, you gain wisdom, strength, and discernment to make it through situations you may have struggled with in the past. God makes a way for His people. However, you must try God. Taste and see that He is indeed the best thing for you in any given situation.

Just as food replenishes us daily, boosts our energy, and gives us the strength to make it through another day,

Jesus does that and so much more. Jesus is our bread and our water. He is the beginning and the ending. He is the truth and the way. Jesus is the ultimate answer to every thinkable question. While you may feed off different foods daily with various dietary restrictions to get your protein, carbohydrates, calcium, sodium, sugar, and fiber intake, God is the one source for all your spiritual dietary needs. Try Jesus, The Lord is more than good.

Ch. 16
Are You Obedient to God?

Would you blatantly ignore God? Would you purposely do what He told you not to do or not do what He told you to do? Sitting back and thinking about it, you may realize you are guilty of being disobedient to God. Or maybe it was just me. That job God did not want you to have but you went for it anyway because it was more money. That new car God told you not to get but you negotiated such a great deal with the salesman. That person God told you to minister to in the grocery store, but you were too scared that person would not accept a word from you. That family in need God told you to bless, but you only had enough money for lunch all week. If you can admit to yourself that one of these or something similar, is you, you can admit that you have not always been obedient to God. And just to be transparent, these are all my examples. I am not playing perfect. But because it happened to me, I know others have been at that crossroad as well.

Of course, I have been disobedient. Let me count the ways. If you have been reading this, basically every relationship I was in went against what God told me. Keep reading, it gets worse. I have gone out and had amazing times all the while praying that God covers me after He warned me to stay home to study, get in my Word, make my financial plan, or simply rest. I was young and vibrant and refused to be held back. Silly me.

As you may have noticed by now, being disobedient to our Heavenly Father can come with consequences. The bible says to be doers of the word, and not hearers only, deceiving yourself. (James 1:22 ESV). Taking that job could have made you miss out on an even better job down the line. Getting that new car could have drastically affected your credit score resulting in you not being able to lease that new apartment or get financed for a new house. Because you did not minister to that person in the store, they cried through the rest of the night not feeling worthy of love. That family you could not help because you could not spare a couple lunches with your buddies is going yet another night without food. All of these could possibly be outcomes in situations when we are not obedient to God. My prayer and belief are that God used another vessel. However, I want to be able to say, "Send me, Lord," and mean it.

And I know you are probably saying, "How do I even know it is God telling me to do this thing or telling me not to do that thing?" While I cannot tell you verbatim each time God has spoken to you, I can certainly tell you that if you pray to God about it, He will surely reveal Himself to you. (James 1:5). There are varies ways He comes to us. God can speak to you through music. You have prayed about a situation and waiting to hear back from God. The lyrics in the song gives you a bold answer that immediately takes you back to the situation you prayed about. Deep inside you know that was God speaking through those lyrics directly to you. God can speak to you through your pastor. (Proverbs 12:15). There have been many days during the sermon I have said to myself, "Man I wish bishop would stay out my business." The Lord has given him a word to give to the people. While it may mean something different to everyone, you will know exactly what part of the message is specifically pertaining to that situation you prayed to God about. God also speaks to us through other people. The Lord will send laborers to do His work. (Matthew 9:38). A friend, a classmate, a co-worker, a therapist, a church member, or even a fellow shopper who is a stranger could be sent by God to tell you something very particular. (Proverbs 15:22). When you hear it, you may want to take a step back a little in disbelief. It will be what you have already discussed with God, and He will send you a confirming message. Understand that the Lord has given that person a message to give to you. God also comes to us as an audible voice. Some people have a very hard time believing that God can come to them in an audible voice. It is not for everyone. When I heard God's voice it was almost a year after I was a licensed attorney. I had only been able to get contract work, and times were hard. Eli and my daddy were basically paying my bills and I told God I would sleep in my car before I went to Eli for anything else. I knew he would help because that is how he was, but I did not want to be rescued like some damsel in distress. And Daddy had enough to worry about with my sister and her twins. Randomly one day I got a call from someone who said she received my resume and thought I would be a good fit at this law firm. I had no recollection of ever submitting a resume, but I listened earnestly. The call turned into an on-the-spot interview, and I was expected to hear back from her by Monday. It was a Friday. I was thanking God for this blessing, but remembered I never applied for the job. I reached for my laptop to search for a real job because clearly this was a scam. At that point, I heard a meek, yet firm, voice asks, "Do you not trust Me?" No doubt I knew it was God. I put down my laptop and was in awe. I started that law firm job soon after.

God comes to You how He knows you will receive Him. He knows each of us better than we know ourselves. However, if you have not heard from God in any facet, that could mean you need to turn some things off around you. (Isaiah 55:3). Those things could be Netflix, social media, inappropriate music, people who mean you no good, your rambling mind that will not allow you to think realistically about a situation. Any of those things could have too much of an impact in your life where it is seriously standing in the way of you hearing God's voice. He is not loud. He will not fight for your attention. He does not have this massive yet amazing James Earl Jones voice that people regularly equate with the voice of Jesus. When you hear Him, you will know that meek, peaceful voice is none other than your God. Most times, God speaks through His Holy Spirit. (Romans 8:26-17). If you have ever had a time when you asked God to show you a thing, when it happened there is something in your conscious saying *that's the sign you asked God for.* You may call it a gut feeling or intuition, but many times that is the Holy Spirit guiding you. The good thing is the more we get in the Word (2 Timothy 3:16) and the more we listen to God (John 10:27), the more recognizable God's voice will be, and you will easily follow Him (John 10:4).

Often, we simply ignore all the signs. I mean, we have all been there just as we do a rolling stop at the stop sign or speed through a yellow light just as it turns red. Yes, God saw that. Instead of wanting to believe the sign is really God, we ask for another sign. God gives it and that is still not enough for us. We need another one. When we get that sign, we ask God for yet another sign. This usually happens when God has told you *no*. Your desires are not lined up with the desires of Christ and you have a hard time accepting it. (Galatians 5:16-17). You are hoping and wishing that this is not the final sign from God. But each time He shows you in an even bolder way. Still, you are reluctant to embrace that answer from God. We go about our lives trying to drown out what God has revealed. You feel if you do not accept that was God speaking to you then you can pretend you did not know. We have all done that. I am guilty of doing that as well.

At one point I was very active on Twitter telling all my business. It was during some trying times one of them being the Eli breakup era. While I was out the picture by being in another state, I was still constantly conversing with him and still watching the other girl's Twitter feed like crazy. Every time she mentioned him was like a dagger in my belly. It was so tormenting. I remember the Lord telling me to stop Twitter stalking Eli's girlfriend because it was only hurting me. He wanted me to truly move on because that relationship was not ordained by Him in the first place. I would be doing so well and out of nowhere I would say well let me just check it out. I would see something I did not want to see and get all upset. My entire mood would change. I felt like I had a setback and had to start over yet again. Yet, we must not react like this when we know God has spoken. We must react like the people of Mizpah saying, "Whether it is pleasing or displeasing, we will obey the voice we will obey the voice of the Lord our God...that it may be will with us when we obey the voice of the Lord our God." (Jeremiah 42:6 NKJV).

When we ignore the things God tells us we are standing in our own way. God is giving you the *no* or the *go ahead* for a particular purpose. When you decide for yourself to go off the path Jesus set out for you, it elongates the process of God fulfilling the promises He has made to you. You can run as much as you want to, but in the end, God will have His way.

Think about the story of Jonah for a minute. God told Jonah to go to Nineveh and to minister to these people so they would not be destroyed for their sins. Jonah was not willing to do this because the people of Nineveh were enemies to Jonah and the people of Israel. (Jonah 1-3). He was thinking *I cannot do this. God is requesting too much from me. They are not my friends, they are enemies. Surely if I do what He is telling me to do these people will live and not die.* Jonah decided to do what he felt would save him, pretend that what God told him was a nonfactor and go away so that God could not find him. Of course, God showed Jonah. Jonah's disobedience was about to get an entire ship of people killed. Jonah knew it was God, and he knew what he had to do. While he was in the belly of the large fish, he came to terms that he must listen to God even when it is something he does not particular want to do. He quickly repented and asked God to forgive him. He had to understand that God would get him through anything that he leads him to. When he got the next chance, he was sure to be obedient to God. His obedience saved an entire people. Those people in Nineveh turned from their evil ways and followed God.

Our obedience to Christ is not only for us. When God tells us to do something or not to do something, know that He has more than you in His plans. Just how your disobedience can come with consequences, your obedience comes with even better outcomes for those God intended it for. When I trusted that God had landed me a position I had never applied for, it opened the door to my first permanent position after being a licensed attorney. I met an amazing woman who worked in HR, and she is still my good friend today. Not to mention I did not have to resort to sleeping in my car as I was able to pay my own bills without help from my daddy or Eli. Remember that if you are willing and obedient, you shall eat the good of the land. (Isaiah 1:19 NKJV).

At times we hear God, and we recognize it is Him no matter how He came to us. Still, we are slow to move when He is very specific as to what He wants us to do. In Acts, Felix was afraid so he told Paul when there is a convenient time that he will call for him. (Acts 24:25). There are so many occasions when we procrastinate. We do it with that paper that we know is due in two weeks. We do it with those bills that need to be sorted by the first of the month. We do it with the weekly tasks we know we must do at home and work. And unfortunately, we procrastinate when we have been given a directive from God. If you are not aware of this yet, know that intentional procrastination is also disobedience to the Father. Even if you are scared to move, even if you are afraid to start that project, or fearful to take that first step, God has commanded that you do it. Do you not realize that if He has led you to it, He will get you through it? You must trust that God is giving you this thing for a reason.

When God first told me to write this book, I was extremely excited. But I was hesitant to move forward when I started thinking about editors, publishers, marketing, and all those other things that must happen to get a book to the masses. The actual work is not fun, God was very specific with what He told me to do. Yet, I found excuses and procrastinated whenever possible. The Lord came back to me and made it clear that I need not worry about all those post writing things at that time. He only told me to write. My reasoning for being so hesitant was because I was afraid. Afraid I would fail, others would judge me, or worst, pity my life. However, I did not let that fear consume me (obviously since you are reading this) but please believe this is years in the making. Proverbs 3:5 reminds us to trust in the Lord with all our hearts and not to lean on our own understanding. Our human nature will have us to believe only what we see. I had to pray. I had to do pep talks. I had to write when my flesh wanted to watch my favorite show or sleep. As humans it is natural to be afraid. But we must not allow that fear to paralyze us. And we surely cannot allow that fear to block our blessing or worse blocking the blessing we have for others.

The next time you are considering ignoring God or being disobedient, think about the possible long-term effect of your decision. Samuel tells us that obedience is better than sacrifice. (1 Samuel 15:22). Not only that, think about how God trusts you with such a task. Our goal is to honor and glorify God with our lives. He does not need us, but He wants us. That is such an honor. We must let go of our own personal desires when they do not line up with the desires God has for us. In the end, you will be glad you were obedient to God.

Ch. 17
To Be Bitter or to Be Better

I have mentioned to you all before that music ministers to me. I know we all hear the Lord differently. He comes to us in incredibly unique ways based on the individual. When I am seeking a revelation or confirmation from Christ, He comes to me a lot in the music that I listen to. While He has come to me through my dreams, bishop's sermons, friends, a tug on my heart, and even audible voice, God knows that music is the way to reach me. Although I am musically challenged myself, I absolutely love music and it takes me to another place, to paradise even. I will sing in the car, shower, even karaoke if the spirits move me, but I was not given any musical talents. Praise God my Calvin has enough for the both of us.

I used to listen to rap music on my own. Eminem is my favorite rapper and I have others I loved such as Tupac, Yo Gotti, and Drake just to name a few. After doing a 31 day fast from secular music, I no longer had a desire for rap. The Lord removed that from me because of the messages I received from the music, the moods the music would put me in, and the overall impact it had on my life. For a while, I literally had no desire to listen to rap music. All rap music did not affect me negatively, but the music I was listening to was not healthy for my spiritual growth. So, I completely stopped listening. The Lord cleaned me up and made me anew. I was so thankful. That rap music that once added to my anger, sadness, or increased sexual desires was all gone.

This is not me telling anyone the music you listen to is sending you to hell. That is not my belief at all. I am also not saying get rid of the rap, rock, R&B, or anything that you feel you can relate to musically. I know music has a connection like no other form of art. I do believe music is our universal language and it has the power to bring complete strangers together. However, for me, the rap was doing more harm than good. It took me to a dark place. My mind is constantly working. What I was allowing in musically had one of the strongest impacts on my thoughts. Because God ministered to me through music, please believe the devil used music to get to me as well. If he wanted me to have an attitude for no reason or wanted me to cry hysterically over past hurt or even wanted me angry at myself and those around me, he knew exactly what type of rap to tap into my spirit. He knew the lyrics and artists that would impact me the most. I let lyrics control my mood until God said no more. Knowing that God cared enough to say no more meant I was special to Him. He was growing me. At that time, I could not allow my personal love for cocaine music to hinder my growth.

Like all things, after God has removed a hinderance, you are tested to see your level of faith. At some point the desire to listen to rap started creeping back in. I refused to let my flesh win yet another battle. I was not sure if I were strong enough to Drake and drive just yet without sending a very toxic text to an ex. I wanted to completely remove all those unhealthy desires from my mind. Matthew 12:43 -45 in the Message version says, "When a defiling evil spirit expelled from someone, it drifts along through the desert looking for an oasis, some unsuspecting soul it can bedevil. When it does not find anyone, it says, 'I'll go back to my old haunt.' On return it finds the person spotlessly clean, but vacant. It then runs out and rounds up seven other spirits more evil than itself and they all move in, whooping it up. That person ends up far worse off than if he'd never gotten cleaned up in the first place." I realized I had not filled that void with anything. When I stopped listening to gangster rap, I did not replace the music with something pure. I was just empty. That is why the desire came back so easily. With my love of music, I knew I would have to find something I enjoyed that also would not make me think I could "make fifty off of three point five." I still have no idea what that means, but I am sure the entire vibe I got listening to that song was not the direction my God was leading me. When those desires to play the latest rap tune came upon me, I knew I needed to do something before I was worse off than before. And Satan was up to his old schemes. He knew it would not take long before I went to an old faithful artist to play the latest tunes.

Neal, a friend of mine who was also extraordinarily strong in his faith, suggested gospel rap music. On a weekend trip home one holiday, Neal played a variety of artists for me. I realized I loved it. Just like the Holy Spirit would touch me listening to Hillsong, Bishop Paul S. Morton, Tasha Cobbs, or Wess Morgan, the Holy Spirit began speaking to me through Mali Music, KB, Lecrae, Trip Lee, and others. I knew this new rap outlet was from God. If I had not replaced that bad spirit with something pure, that spirit was going to come back stronger than ever to influence me negatively. I thank God for allowing that friend to open my heart and mind to something different that was pleasing to God.

As I was driving home from the gym one day, I decided to continue playing the music I was listening to while at the gym. I had the KB station playing from Pandora. A song from Andy Mineo began playing. I have heard this artist numerous times, but this song was new to me. It instantly caught my attention. Mineo sang about rejection, un-forgiveness, grudges, and hypocrites. He discussed how he reacted when his father would call him now although they had never been close. His father was not always there, and he sometimes still thinks about that impact. He stated that bitterness was a choice. While my relationship with my father was awesome, I instantly started thinking about the relationship, or lack thereof, I had with my mom.

My mother and I are not as close as I would like. I must admit, I have always desired to have that storybook mother daughter relationship where the mom is the daughter's everything and go-to for anything. When my father started to take on that role because he noticed I desired that relationship, I sort of desired it less with my mom. However, as a young woman I could not be as candid with my father and there were more than a few times I longed for that relationship with my mom. I thank God for Him being a mother and a father to me. He was everything to me and has been since I completely gave my life over to Him a few years ago. Yet, I can see a call or text from my mother, and I roll my eyes before answering or responding. I wish I could blame this on the fact that it was her call that informed me that my father had been murdered, but I felt this way beforehand. I constantly told myself that I had forgiven my mom for not being there those times I needed her. I prayed to God and asked Him to forgive her and to restore our relationship. I had even gotten to a point in Christ that if my relationship with my mother had never been entirely restored, I would still be okay.

The rolling of my eyes when I saw "Mama" come across my screen said differently. Seeing the phone ringing and opting to call back at another time spoke volumes. I was still bitter. That is not a place where I wanted to be at all. When Lecrae said, "They say 'Don't get bitter, get better.' I'm working on switching them letters," I felt that. I needed to get better, not bitter. I could not blame my bitterness on anyone else at this point. I had done the work in other areas before. God was working on me and through me. I had to work through these tougher situations and be true to myself and to God.

Tears began to well up in my eyes. I could not believe I was a hypocrite. I preached to friends and family about forgiveness. I posted on my social media about being a hearer and doer of the word. Jesus said, "These people honor me with their lips, butt their hearts are far from me." (Matthew 15:8). And here I was, bitter. I had the choice not to be bitter; I could have chosen to be better. I could have chosen to forgive. But here I was holding a grudge based on the rejection I felt from my mom for years. It was not exemplary of me as a child of God. I prayed this prayer:

Lord, please forgive me. All this time I kept telling myself I had forgiven her. All the times I had asked you to forgive her and to help me forgive. I truly thought it was gone. I realize now that I am still harboring impure thoughts. I am sorry, Lord. I know that I cannot ask for something of You when I am not willing to give it myself. Lord, I do not want to be bitter. I do not want to be a hypocrite. Lord, I love my mother with everything in me. Continue working on her; continue working on me. Without her there would be no me. Lord, I thank you for her. I thank You for forgiving her. I asked that you create in me a clean heart where I can truly be better. Make me better, make me more like You. Remove everything in me that is not of You. My desire is not to be bitter, my desire is to be a better Christian, a better daughter, and better in every way through Christ. Lord this and all things I pray in Your wonderful Son Jesus' mighty name. Amen, amen, and amen.

Admitting I had not fully forgiven my mom was hard. But praying that sincere prayer let me know that I was not holding a grudge and I was not being a hypocrite. I genuinely wanted to forgive. Instead of being bitter, I thank God that I am now coming to terms that change does not come over night. Some things will always be a work in progress. He who began a good work in you will carry it on to completion until the day of Jesus Christ (Philippians 1:6 NIV). If it takes God working on me day in and day out until the return of Christ, I know that He is still with me. I decided to look at all the positives I had in having a mom. I found ways to smile about how she taught me the power of prayer. I know my relationship with God started with the seed she planted in me at such a young age. My mother gave me the best gift of all.

We all have different stories, backgrounds, childhoods, and even adulthoods. While letting go of bitterness toward my mom was such a huge duty, you may not have that issue. You may have that cookie cutter relationship with mom. That is a blessing. Some no longer have their earthly parents. May God continue to be with you. Others are dealing with bitterness stimming from completely different areas or subject matters. Whatever it is, know that bitterness is a choice. When you choose to let your emotions control you, you are also choosing not to allow the Holy Spirit to lead you. Ephesians let all bitterness...be put away from you, with all malice; and be kind to one another, tenderhearted, forgiving one another, even as God in Christ forgave you (Ephesians 4:31-32 NKJV).

That bitterness that is stopping you from being better in Christ, let it go. Do not be dismayed if this is not a rapid process. Trust the process. Trust God. Document your growth. Since it is gradual, it will be hard to see in real time. If you write it out, or find a way to document your steps, you will see how far you have come. If it is something you truly desire, the Lord already knows it. Take it to Him. Let Him work on you. It is such an amazing feeling when you know God is working on you. It makes you feel so special. He is giving little me the time of day and He is truly making me better. Just as God has forgiven us for our many iniquities, we must learn to do the same for others. And it is not for that person, it is for you. The prayer I prayed may not be the prayer that helps you get to better. If it is, be my guest and use it as much as you need to use it. If not, do not hesitate to say the prayer you need to say to let go of grudges, bitterness, and unforgiveness. It can be as simple as this:

God, I thought I had forgiven [insert name here] for _____, but I have detected bitterness in my heart, Lord. Please remove that bitterness and any grudges I have toward [insert name here]. Lord, allow me to completely forgive and to completely heal. Give me the steps. Allow me to trust You in the process. Thank You in advance because I know that it is already done in Your Son Jesus' Mighty Name.

The work is not overnight. It takes time. You may have to pray the prayer every day, a few times a day. If you genuinely believe and have the desire to move forward, you will. God hears you. God knows that you truly desire to live a life for Him. Add this to the list of things God is going to work out in your favor because the favor of God is on your life. As the song says, "Life can leave you so bitter, but you must believe it gets better. It's alright, dry your eyes, and send a prayer to the skies. I know it's hard to fight, but you must believe. It gets better."

I thank God that He put a new song in my heart. I may not have ever come to terms with my anger and bitterness had I kept listening to lyrics that was magnifying those very emotions. As much as I love me some Eminem, that whole "if you try to leave me again, I will tie you to the bed and set the house on fire" is not the space for me. I was bitter when Eli told me via text that he was no longer in love with me. At the time, he was not in love with anyone. I knew it was soon to be the same person who caused our breakup just a year or so beforehand. I felt a million different emotions. In the end, God told me to pray for them. I was like hold up God. You want me to do what? I was not in the business of praying for people who dragged my name in the mud or who hurt me and felt a text was the appropriate way to express feelings. Forget that. I was not praying for them. God had me confused with someone more like Him. I was not there yet. Yes, I was trying to be like Christ, but it was too much Page and Jones (my parents' last names) in me.

God kept dropping it in my spirit to pray for Eli and his now girlfriend. The girl who was the other woman at one point, then became the only woman while I had to deal with my own brokenness. He told me if I truly wanted to be better, I had to literally be better. God is so right. Literally all the time. I was simply not feeling the "be right" life at the time. After fighting it for weeks, I got on my face and prayed. I prayed for her, him, and them both individually and collectively. I knew he had struggles I was not able to be there for as a friend or a girlfriend. I knew she was a single mother of three kids and was doing the best that she could like every great mom. I prayed that they grew together and followed God's will for their lives. I prayed God's best for them in all aspects of their lives. Everyone has battles and no matter how I felt about what happened to that relationship, if I wanted to learn and grow from it, I could not allow me to be bitter. I was still hopeful for God's best and God had already told me that Eli was not in His plans for me. It was my fault I stayed longer than I should have.

It was not until God told me to do a new thing that I started being able to heal from the inside out. The new song gave me a new perspective. Music may not have this strong of an impact on you. It may not affect you at all. Whatever your thing is that you think is helping you get through what you are dealing with, if it is not of God and you know it, I challenge you to take a fast from it. Replace it with something that you know is of God. Let him lead you. I cannot wait to see how it changes your thought process. Remember, it is a process. This takes time and that is to be expected.

Ch. 18
Walk by Faith not by Sight

I am nearsighted. That means I have a hard time seeing things further away. My eyes do not focus as they should, and those objects appear blurry. I remember going to the eye doctor as a teenager and being told my sight would worsen as I got older but if I wore glasses or contact lenses at that time, my sight would worsen quicker. I decided against both. My father always bragged about his 20/20 vision. I wanted to have that keen vision as well, so I never owned up to the problems I started to have in my late 20s. Once Daddy passed, I began to see it was time to do what was best for my eyes. I remember being at my grandmother's house and me asking her and my aunt why the TV was so blurry, and I even suggested she get a new TV. My grandmother and aunt were so confused. They felt nothing was wrong with the recently bought TV. An old friend came over and I asked her was she able to see the screen clearly. She said everything was fine to her. Could I be the only crazy person? I had noticed more I more I had to ask my neighbor at church what was the verse on the jumbo screen, and I could see no facial features on the choir members. The last straw was when I ran over a median leaving the grocery. Enough was enough; I got a couple cute frames and corrective lenses.

One Sunday, Palm Sunday to be exact, I had a calendar full of things to do. First stop was church for Sunday school and service. In Sunday school, I could not see the board without my glasses. Our teacher for the day had placed specific verses on the board so it was imperative I could see. I pulled out my handy, dandy glasses and put them on. Once I got in the sanctuary, I already knew I would not be able to see anything in the pulpit or back. I would not have seen the praise team, the choir, the large screens, or even bishop. I figured it was best I kept my glasses on. I had errands to run after church. I needed my glasses obviously to see during this time. I went to work out before going home to make dinner. I wore my glasses during most of the class. The instructor announced during the next song there would be planks. I couldn't risk my glasses falling off my face. I took them off for all of four minutes. This was the worse four minutes of my day. Everything was a blur to me. I continued moving because I did not want my heartrate to drop just yet, but it was a struggle. As I moved around to a routine I was not as familiar with, I could barely see my instructor give direction. But I did not put my glasses back on. I knew the planks were coming soon and breaking my glasses was not an option. We did the planks. It was like a whirlwind. As soon as we finished, I inched back over to put my glasses on. As I drove home, I got frustrated at my need for my glasses. I did not like to depend on other things for correction. I wanted to be able to see without the help of these lenses. While at a stoplight, I took the glasses off and placed them in my purse. When the light turned green, I looked up to see I could not even make out the name of the street. At the top of my lungs I yelled, "UGH! Lord why don't You just heal my eyes so I don't need these glasses; I know You can." I am so bold. I talk to God just like I talk to my friends because that is who He is to me. But I was no fool. I slowly reached over to my bag to get my glasses out. The corrective lenses were necessary if I wanted to make it home safely. As I drove the 28 minutes home, the Lord revealed some things to me.

First, God fixed the problem how He saw fit to fix the problem. He who made a way through the sea, a path through the mighty water; I am making a way in the wilderness and streams in the wasteland. (Isaiah 43:16,19 NIV). There is nothing God cannot do; however, when He does something contrary to our standards, we are unappreciative. Not to mention we are undeserving of His goodness, kindness, and mercy yet He still gives freely. Too often we ask for His help, but we want a different kind of solution. We fall on our face daily asking the Lord to move, to show Himself, to use us, to have His way. We go to Him for a lot. God finally manifests. He moves, He shows us just who He is, He uses us like never before, and He has His way in every part of our lives. Then eventually, we are unhappy and dissatisfied. We are even ashamed to admit that we are displeased with what God has done because it is no longer enough, because we are too far removed that we cannot remember the place He rescued us from, or because we are in a society that embraces stuff we want more.

We must have faith that God knows exactly what He is doing. 1 Corinthians 2:5 NIV says so that your faith might not rest on human wisdom, but on God's power. There is no doubt that at least once in our lifetimes we felt we had the answer. Then God came and showed us another way. Consider Proverbs 3:5 and trust and believe the way He shows you. Our intellect is limited, His is infinite. At that moment we may not have been excited about the way God showed us. However, once we were removed from the situation, we begin to appreciate just how amazing God is and how much He loves us. He may bring us through our storm in a very unconventional way. Furthermore, He may change us in our storm. For my thoughts are not your thoughts, nor are your ways My ways, says the Lord. (Isaiah 55:8 NKJV). We cannot expect God to be on our level and have a "right now" mindset when He moves in our lives. We may be thinking long term on this earth; however, God is thinking eternity. "For as the heavens are higher than the earth, so are My ways higher than your ways, and My thoughts than your thoughts. (Isaiah 55:9 NKJV).

Princess Page Rogers

When we have planned our lives out to perfection, or when we have decided to go with the flow of wherever the Lord takes us, there may come (or has come) about a time when you tried to tell God what was best for you. *No God... wait. I know I said move but I really wanted to go east to this job, to this career, to this school, to this mate. I did not mean move by taking me this other way doing a job like this, or getting accepted to this graduate program, or not spending the rest of my life with my high school sweetheart. Start over God and move again.*

I know I said show me who You are, and I see that you are a great God and Father, but I am still not ready just yet to fully submit because.... Although You have shown me You, how do I know it's really You? I will stay doing me for now. I need more signs that it is You.

Lord, when I said use me, I wanted you to make me a missionary so all would know my name while I do work in my city. I did not want to go oversees in a developing country with no running water or Wi-Fi in the home. There are so many people who need you right here God. So, use me right here where I am.

Lord I know I said have your way, but did You mean for me to deal with this death, this illness, this financial fall? Are You mad at me? Do You even love me?

These are just examples of what we say to God after He has done everything we prayed and asked Him to do. Yet, it was not the result we wanted so there is an issue with it. The Lord does His work in us, not the works we have picked out for ourselves. (Philippians 1:6).

It is important to know that we cannot pray to God about a situation and then expect our own solution. Praise God that His ways and thoughts are higher than ours. While we are considering the next few years, God is looking beyond this lifetime. I prayed to regain sight. God gave me a new pair of glasses. Without those glasses, my sight is still subpar. Once I actually utilize those corrective lenses, my sight is now exceptional. If you rely on your own solutions for your life, you will continue living a subpar life. As soon as you accept the direction and results from the Lord, you will move into your destiny which consists of an exceptional life. Issues and hard times will still come, but God's framework is being utilized and you now see just how bright your future will be.

The Lord also showed me I needed His correction. I cannot do it alone. Whoever ignores instruction despises himself, but he who listens to reproof gains intelligence (Proverbs 15:32 ESV). I was becoming someone who neglected my own need. I did not want the proper correction the Lord put in front of me. Here I am able to see everything clearly, but because it is not the result I desire, I was choosing to remain in the dark. Once I allowed my glasses to do the exact thing they were made to do, I could see. I understood all the things around me. Those lenses were a gift from God. He corrected my sight and gave me the sight I was lacking.

There have been other areas in my life where God had to straighten me up. God had to come in and completely remove me from situations. His correction was His way of showing me His love. (Hebrews 12:6). And I know that without Him stepping in I would not have made it out of those trying times. I plan out everything. Literally everything because I need that organization in my life. I use an actual planner, not my phone so I can write out my schedule. I have a to-do list that I make every day for work. It reminds me of my tasks and checking off those tasks are just as important as accomplishing them. I plan my birthday two months in advance, but I do not tell people until a month, so they are not overwhelmed by my promptness. Calvin and I planned to get pregnant after my thirty-fifth birthday. I have inherited uterine fibroids, non-cancerous tumors that develop in the uterus during a woman's childbearing ages. These fibroids have been like carrying a child. They sit on my bladder, I literally look four months pregnant if I am not working my angles, and they make it completely uncomfortable to lie flat on my stomach. I knew there may be some minor complications with pregnancy, but I also knew there was nothing too big for my God. I went to my gynecologist a month before my thirty-fifth birthday knowing the fibroids had grown due to the growth in my stomach, but I was also being hopeful. I brought God with me. I had prayed His will, and I knew He was going to look out for His girl, me. Well, after the ultrasound, I learned not only had my fibroids grown, but I had two additional ones come join the party in my uterus. The placement and the size of these noncancerous tumors caused my doctor to give me her professional opinion that the best method of removal, to allow me to get pregnant and then to carry a healthy baby full-term, was to have a myomectomy cutting across my bikini line to open me up. I completely zoned out in that room thinking God, I thought I said show up. What are you even doing? I begin thinking maybe having a baby is not for me. It's too much work. This world is too crazy anyway. After crying hysterically for hours like the infant child I could not naturally have, I centered myself. I put on my gospel music because it gives what needs to be given. And I needed all of that. God did what only He could do. He slipped in my spirit that delay is not a denial. He also told me to be realistic that me being upset and hurt is mostly because I had a timeline and I now see that that thing will not go my way. Y'all, Jesus really comes with all the audacity. And again, He is always right. Had I gotten pregnant right after I turned thirty-five, I could have a summer baby still age thirty-five, and be ready to get my body back come thirty-six. It is never about me; it is never about you. God will show Himself. We must be willing to move out the way, use those corrective lenses, and allow

God to lead the way. I had to take my faith into overload.

Sometimes you do not know you cannot see until you get corrective lenses. You may think this is just the way things are or you may be like me and think everyone around you is the one with the issue. The entire time I did not have my corrective lenses, I was okay with living a blurred life. I knew I had to move closer to see. I knew being further away meant not making out the details. However, it took the corrective lenses for me to know my sight was impaired. They showed me what I was missing. The clarity was missing. The details were missing. The indentions were missing. When I started to see clearly, it transformed other things in my life. Once you get your sight, you will not want to stay in the dark. (Proverbs 13:9). You will want to see the beauty you have missed on God's timeline, not your own.

Ch. 19
In My Bag

I mentioned I am from Memphis, Tennessee, born and raised, but I have resided in Nashville, Tennessee since the last quarter of 2012. I am always up and down Interstate 40 to and from Memphis. I am a last-minute packer. Last minute to the point of I will pack an hour before it is time for me to leave. However, I am typically good about organization. My clothes are folded nice and neat. Everything has a particular place, and each item is in that place. I learned that sometimes the way you pack your bag can determine how heavy the bag is. One weekend I was traveling from Nashville to Memphis. On this occasion I packed lighter than normal, but I carried the same size weekend bag I carry on the regular. Because of the way I had the clothes, shoes, and toiletries packed in, the bag was particularly light. While home I ate a lot of good food. I had my grandmama's homemade biscuits, Memphis style hot wings, and a host of other things I mostly want to keep to myself just thinking about how much I indulged during this short time frame. I am truly a lover of food. Trust me, I eat the most while home, but it is usually the unhealthy foods because I am "vacationing" and "deserve it." I mustered up the strength to get out of the bed at my aunt's house and prepare to get back on the road Sunday morning. When I packed up to head back to Nashville, I noticed the exact same bag with the exact same things in it was a lot heavier this time around. The difference was I did not take the time to nicely fold and organize the items in my weekend bag. I simply threw things in and mushed it together until the bag closed. I did not want to spend the necessary time it took to put everything in its respective place. Because of that, I had a mess of a bag that I had to force to zip to the point that my fingers were red from the constant pinching after forcefully fighting my bag to close.

Sadly, this is something we all do in life. Well, let me rephrase. I do not know your life. However, I know my own. I know I have been guilty of handling my life the way I handled my bag. When I have an endless amount of things going on and cannot focus on one; when I feel like time is getting the best of me; when I am overwhelmed with the tasks on my to do list; when I am on an emotional rollercoaster; when I know I am doing all I can do, yet it is still not enough; when I know there is literally nothing I can do to fix a problem I so want to fix; and when I am completely drained from putting everyone else's feelings above my own, I am a cluttered, disorganized mess.

There is something that makes all of us discombobulated. I am sure it varies for each of us because we are all unique beings. And we all have our own way of dealing with being flustered, frustrated, or even fearful. My way is dumping it all in my bag with complete disregard because taking the time to organize and go through each detail is too much for me. I know this is not a good way to deal. I know avoidance comes with destruction in the end if I am not careful. I also know eventually I must take everything out the bag even if it is simply to reuse the bag. So, at some point I must face the music.

I will not be the person to tell you to deal with all those issues at once. I will not say if you do not deal with every single issue when you are packing the bag you are causing a bigger problem in the end. That is, absolutely, not who I am. I am the person who says stuff that bag girl. Push it in deeper and deeper. Sit on it if need be; ensure it closes. Nobody has time to deal with all that baggage especially not on the closeout of a visit that is supposed to be serene. Is this good or bad advice? For me, I cannot deal with my issues until I am ready to do so. I sincerely know issues need to be dealt with in a timely manner. I know it is important to focus on any and every issue that can result in anxiety, uneasiness, and the feeling of being overwhelmed or out of control. I also know that it cannot be taken lightly. I do not recommend trying to unpack, figuratively and literally, this bag alone.

Take every piece to God. Gives it to the One who will handle each garment with care. Isaiah says I will be your God throughout your lifetime—until your hair is white with age. I made you, and I will care for you. I will carry you along and save you (Isaiah 46:4 NLT). God wants us to bring everything to Him. The Lord made us. He knows we are far from perfect. He still wants us to seek comfort in Him. His Word says, "I have seen what they do, but I will heal them anyway! I will lead them. I will comfort…." (Isaiah 57:18 NLT). It is the *anyway* for me! I felt that because He knows we messed up. He knows we are messy. He knows we possibly caused some of our own issues. He knows we have been petty. He knows we let that bag fill to the top with discourse when we knew there was a better way. He still loves us and still cares for us. When you allow God to unpack your bag, He will bring you peace. God gives his people peace. (Psalm 29:11 MSG). [He] will keep in perfect peace all who trust in [Him], and whose thoughts are fixed on [Him]! Isaiah (26:3 NLT).

I will pull one from the young people. Gen Z and even some of my fellow millennials love to say they are "in their bag." I stroll through social media and every other caption is "in my bag" to let people know they are working aimlessly to complete a certain task. What "in my bag" essentially translate to is that a person is focused and determined on a specific goal. When I am in my bag, I refuse to let the slightest thing get me down. I can have all the same issues I mentioned earlier; however, the Lord prepared me. My focus, determination, and inability to quit did not come from me. I am in my bag because God kept me and comforted me through it all.

You must first go in your bag, unpack, allow God to work, to in turn be "in your bag." No matter how much you say you are focused and determined, if you have not allowed God to do the work, you are not maximizing your full potential. Take me for instance. After all, this is about me since I do not know your life. When God placed this book in my spirit years before I finished, I was so ecstatic I told the world. No, I seriously told the world. I got on all my social media platforms making a grandiose announcement. All but Snap Chat since it only lasts 24 hours anyway what was the point. I knew God told me to write so why not tell the world. How about because God did not release me to tell the world. I should have been discrete and moved in silence. After that, many distractions came. All the work of the enemy allowed me to lose focus. Over the timeframe, many things I refused to unpack. I did not want to address that my lingering feelings for my ex led me down a path of destruction I would have never imagined. I did not want to admit that I felt shame for what others considered successful when there was not anything I could do to make others want success as much as I wanted it for them. How dare I say I felt helpless knowing my brothers whom I would take a bullet for as kids were serving an outrageous amount of time in prison when convicted as minors simply because they could not afford effective legal counsel. All these things started toying at me. So how could I write when the world around me was falling apart. It took God, my therapist, and me willing to do the work to unpack my bag. It was not easy. But I knew to be in my bag how God wanted me to be, I had to let go of so much baggage.

Some of us have little small things that grow into something bigger. Some of us start off with large matters and try to bury them due to them feeling as if they could possibly be the death of us if tackled all at once. No matter what it could be, once that bag gets unorganized and piled to the top, there will be difficulty in closing it. You will struggle. Remember you will have to unpack and de-clutter at some point. My suggestion is to unpack piece by piece with God leading you to peace in Him. We all want to be in our bag. It starts with unpacking all the nonsense or pain in it first.

Ch. 20
Flawless Because of the Cross

Let's all take a moment and simply be honest with ourselves. Although we constantly post our best selfies, most memorable moments, and high points in life on social media, we are not always that confident in ourselves. We have hurt, pain, bad hair days, and days our glow seemed to have stayed home in bed. Sometimes that thing one person said to you about your body, your height, your attire got to you and stuck in your head. It may have made you feel less then. I come to tell you that God's love for you makes you perfect in His eyes.

As humans, we will point out what someone else is wearing, someone else's hair, someone else's features or beauty enhancements. Often, we think we are being helpful. Other times, we are purposely being mean. These acts are not of God no matter how you try to phrase it. God looks at our hearts. (1 Samuel 16:7). I am so thankful the Lord does not see as man. I thank God He is God and not us. In our humanity, we are conditioned to look at the appearance which can do more harm than good. I am not saying do not try to look nice, shower, style or cut your hair. I am saying we should not pass judgment on someone simply because they are wearing white after Labor Day or carrying a knock off bag. That forty-dollar bag or the heels that need a repair could be why someone was able to afford their dream home. The oversized suit could be a result of massive weight lost and the person is still working toward a goal before making any new purchases.

Some may say my eyes are a little larger than average. Ever since I can remember, I was admired because of my eyes. As a little girl one of the family friends would call me Bright Eyes. She said I could light up a room. I always had "eyes" listed as my most appealing feature. A friend of mine always told me my eyes randomly glowed. He said the light would hit my eyes at the right angle at the right time of day, and they sparkled. Of course, all those compliments made me smile. But I also remember another young lady posting horrible comments about me on social media specifically about my eyes making me look like a frog. I pretended that I was not bothered. On the outside I tried to play it off because she had never met me in person so her opinion should have been irrelevant. Sadly, it was relevant to me. I cared. It hurt my feelings that this stranger felt the need to call me out on social media but more importantly felt the need to make an attack on the attribute I felt good about. I second guessed myself numerous times. I took my attitude, my hurt to God. I wanted to know why I was given this daunting trait. Never mind my entire life I was proud to be told I had big, beautiful eyes. Now, at that very moment, I let the words of one cruel individual make me despise this feature.

Sadly, sometimes one negative thing can grab your attention more than a hundred positive things. But if you know the God I serve; you know God did not let me have a pity party. God reminded me that He made no mistakes making me the way He did. According to Jeremiah 1:5, God knew me before He formed me in my mother's womb. If God knew everything about me, He knew every feature.

I read Gabrielle Union's book "We Are Going to Need More Wine." In her book she was open and honest about being a mean girl. She said she felt good about putting other women down who were not present at the time. It took her a minute to realize this was part of her happiness. She was asked by her life coach how it adds to her life and if it changes what she goes home to. That is when she realized bringing other women down could not bring an ounce of happiness to her life.

I had a conversation with a friend discussing the way

women dress. I have always felt that the way you dress is part of who you are. When you have the freedom to pick your own clothes, you can be expressive with what you wear. I work in the legal field. However, we are more business casual than anything. A lot of people push the button to dress it down because they feel more comfortable. I usually come in wearing my heels, a career dress, and a nice blazer to match. The attire I wear makes me feel "ready to work." I can get just as much work done in khakis and a button down, I have done it many times; however, I happen to like heels and dresses.

The conversation moved from the workplace to everyday style of dress. I know most women would love to have the ability to shop and get all their favorite designers and wear their pieces in numerous ways to show your true self. I, on the other hand, can put on an oversized sweatshirt or a Cami top (depending on the weather) with jeans or tights and be good to go. My big sister has all but forced me to wear earrings. I am now seeking earrings out more. I must say, they are a great asset even the clip-ons I am required to wear not having pierced ears. I am not a fashionista. I will never claim to be. While I have been styled by one of the most fashionable women I know, I went back to my boring dresses. In conversation, my friend said, as a feminist, she feels that women should dress however they want and not get the backlash from others. I was thinking that in part, I agree. I think we should all be able to dress in what makes us feel like us, but also understand who we represent. 2 Corinthians 5:20 NKJV says that we are ambassadors of Christ. I never want the way I consider dressing to express myself to make someone else think God does not reside in me. You can be sexy, urban, artistic, goth, flamboyant and on fire for God. However, I was part of the problem. Even though I have never said anything to anyone who dressed differently from me or what appeared to be "too much," I had my thoughts. Sometimes I felt maybe that is all they had. Other times, I was thinking, why be so flashy or why be so extra? I even used scripture to back up my antics. I knew as a wife (even before I was married, I knew I was a wife) I had to dress a certain way. Again, I never tried to dress like anyone but me. I am not a small woman. I wear what I feel comfortable in and what makes me feel pretty. At the same time, I had no reason to speak on another person for how they dressed. No matter what I see, God sees beauty. God sees a heart He loves. God sees His child.

We sometimes speak on people without knowing. On a facetime call, an old friend asked why I would wear braids so long and that if I wanted my hair to grow, I needed to take them out. She said her natural hair was long and healthy, but she refuses to wear it since she feels more comfortable in wigs and weaves. She also advised me not to have daughters if I was not going to ensure they had long pretty hair. I was puzzled, but I said my hair is healthy. I am not a stylist or anything close to it. I have a standing appointment with a stylist I happily pay because hair is not my thing. I have a friend who does sew-ins like a licensed professional and she is a godsend for me and others. I have never been above having someone else care for my hair. I know my ministry and hair is not it for me. Also, I care more about health than I do length. I will quickly cut the length off to keep healthy hair. Yet, we have this vision that long hair is healthy hair. I do not believe my old friend was being shady. She was really trying to help me. It was not helpful. I felt there was another way to say it. Yet, knowing that she has gorgeous hair that she refuses to show, indicates she has a different standard. I thought I wear my hair maybe you should try that. But she does what feels comfortable to her. I do what is comfortable to me. Neither of us are wrong.

I left that call thinking how that conversation and

many other conversations we have as associates could glorify Christ. I realized putting our own impressions on others do not allow people to be their true selves. We do not allow someone to express who they are through the art of what they wear because we want them to conform to what we think is fashionable, classy, acceptable, and so much more. In my dress and blazer someone may not feel comfortable approaching me with wanting to know more about Christ because I may appear as if I already have it together (I do not). In sweats and sneakers, the youth may be acceptable to hearing your story even if an older individual looks the other way. Ephesians 2:10 NIV says we are God's handiwork, created in Christ Jesus to do good works, which God prepared in advance for us to do. You have your style of dress because God has made that a part of who you are.

On one end we are team no makeup. On the other end we are wearing makeup to please ourselves. We can be both. We can want to go barefaced and want to be beat. No one should have an opinion either way. If you are rocking natural hair, relaxed hair, someone else's hair, do it with dignity and pride. If your physical features differ from those of your peers, know that God made you unique for a reason. You are beautiful. With every single imperfection we can find in someone, God has said we are flawless in Him. I took another look at 2 Corinthian 5. This time I read in in the Message version.

> Because of this decision we don't evaluate people by what they have or how they look. We looked at the Messiah that way once and got it all wrong, as you know. We certainly don't look at him that way anymore. Now we look inside, and what we see is that anyone united with the Messiah gets a fresh start, is created new. The old life is gone; a new life burgeons! Look at it! All this comes from the God who settled the relationship between us and him, and then called us to set-

tle our relationships with each other. God put the world square with himself through the Messiah, giving the world a fresh start by offering forgiveness of sins. God has given us the task of telling everyone what he is doing. We're Christ's representatives. God uses us to persuade men and women to drop their differences and enter into God's work of making things right between them. We're speaking for Christ himself now: Become friends with God; he's already a friend with you. (2 Corinthians 5:16-20 MSG).

With God as our friend and us as a friend of God, He is the artist. If He has okayed the fit, the hairstyle, the makeup, the features, no human can change your stance. If you have yet to have that authentic relationship with Christ, trust that once you receive it, God will convict you if you are outside His will even in the shoes you wear. However, God makes us all different for a reason. He has children on every end of this earth that comes in every shade and every size. God wants his ambassadors to look different because His children are different. No two people were made the same. No two people are completely the same. Even for identical twins, they have the same DNA, but something is different about them. And even if on the surface they look the same, they have different personalities. Our differences unite us more than they separate us. Jesus did not die for us to bring each other down for being different. He wants us to embrace the uniqueness and know that He sees us as spotless. (Ephesians 5:27).

Next time you see someone not dressing to your standards, or someone who decided to get some cosmetic work done to feel better about themselves, before you pass judgment, remember the Jesus died for them too. Let them be flawless in those jeans and genes.

Ch. 21
Unapologetically Me

I did not change who I was for what I wanted. I became a better me, I loved me more, I cared for myself more. I was selfish with who I allowed in my space and who was worthy of my time. All the things I loved doing, I did them. Some things I learned along the way of being the better me. I loved those things, so I stayed with it. Dance parties and or praise parties to start the day are absolutely amazing. They truly lift you up and have you feeling amazing as you take on the day.

Other things I did, I realized I did not really care for it. It had become part of a ritual I picked up from someone else or to please someone else. I am a sports fanatic. Not crazy to the point that I am mean to someone who is a fan of a rival team. But I am very much so a fan of the game. I like to watch sports, I listen to sports radio, I follow various sports social media accounts, I have my favorite teams and players on and off the court. One thing I used to do every morning was turn on ESPN to watch Sports Center. I liked to hear sports talk first thing in the morning. It was cool and light; however, at times it put me on defense because I knew I would have to argue my point as to why I agreed or disagreed with the analyst. This is something Eli and I both did at that time. We would listen and talk back to the television or to each other. We had varying views on some things, but for the most part, Eli did not really respect my sports opinion because I am a female. I would say but how can you say that he is the best of all time when his stats do not compare to [insert name with even better stats]. Eli would say it was a different time and the game has changed. While that did help me with a healthy debate in the legal field, it was not what I wanted to do every morning since it instantly put me on defense. Well, the more time I spent becoming a better me and loving on myself, I noticed I did not want to wake up to ESPN every morning. I did not want to turn on the TV at all. The more I thought about it, I watched ESPN every morning and said it was what I wanted since I do genuinely like sports. Yet, it did not make me feel better. I much rather listen to music. It made me feel good. It could lighten me, but it moved me. Some songs would have me praising God while brushing my hair. Other songs will have me dancing while trying to get in my career dress. I still had the option to skim the ESPN app for updates. I could go on Twitter to see what sports analysts were talking about without taking away from my morning music party. That was my new thing just for me. I wanted to be unapologetically me, doing what I love to do.

So many times, I hear women saying they must learn to cook to get a husband. A man says he must make more money before he can seek a wife. While I totally understand wanting to be able to cook for yourself and family, at least the basics, if that is not your thing, the man God has for you will understand. The Lord can place someone in your life who wants to discover the craft with you or even better teach you some recipes. There is nothing like a man teaching you something new. Think about dates when the two of you can learn a dish together. That is something special, memorable, and you have a new skill in the kitchen.

I have always loved cooking. I saw people gathering around eating my food and how happy they seemed. Amid chaos, we had those precious moments to savor over sweet and savory dishes. I wanted to keep that. I was the epitome of single when I started my catering business. I was already practicing law, but I loved cooking in college and law school, so I channeled that into something more. It was a happy place for me. I was not doing it for a man. I did it for me and the love of people. Also, the love of food obviously had a huge impact on my decision. I felt that was obvious, but also did not want to leave out I love to eat more than anyone I know other than my husband. I remember all the men I was preparing gourmet meals for who walked away from me, or I walked away from them. I never want someone to stay or "pick me" because my food is delicious. Yes, my food is good. However, I am a beautiful spirit. I have a huge heart. I am funny at times, and I am passionate, sincere, and genuine. I cannot honestly say a man would stay simply because you cook. You can be top chef and if that man is not the man for you, he is simply not the one for you and that is okay.

I had a conversation with some of my girlfriends because they kept saying things like, I have learned to cook now so where is my husband, now that I have these cooking skills God can bring on my husband, and now I am going to be a good wife since I cook. I simply asked if they believed cooking was required to be a wife in this day. They all said no but followed up with saying I am married, and I cook. Please, do not think the math is mathing in that equation. I cook because I love it. After a long day, I love to cook. It makes me feel good. On Saturdays, I will spend all morning cleaning and all afternoon cooking. I sample different recipes. I can remember asking friends to come over just so I did not have to cook for a party of 1. My actual husband, Calvin, did not marry me for my cooking. He did express he wanted a woman who could cook, but he also was okay with spending most of his money on eating out. He felt he was a good cook as well. I am a living witness that his cooking skills are an inquired taste, but he means well. You may be shocked to know I may have cooked for Calvin twice before he proposed. I can only remember one time, but he says it was twice so I will give him that. It was not about a cooking skill. It was about our connection, our love for God, and love for each other. Of course, the connection including the physical attraction, I will not pretend I was too holy to see his handsomeness with that brown skin and long neatly twisted locs.

Yes, work on being a better you. Do the work. Yes, get over past hurt and trauma. Do the work. But like me, I believe you too are a beautiful spirit with a good heart. Let those things and other characteristics shine. We are all a work in progress. That never means pretending or doing what we loathe or despise to win someone over. Do you really want to pretend for 60-70 years? Let us not fake it until we make it with our spouses. We want them to love us for us. We want our significant other to look at us and say that is all mine and you truly are yourself, not fabricating who you are to get the ring. I am a perfect example that it is better to lose for standing in your truth than to gain because of misrepresentation.

I understand a man is a provider who wants to be able to provide for his wife and family. However, if your lady is only willing to date her because of your tax bracket, does she really love you for you? If you cannot have a Chick Fil a or Chipotle date occasionally then more money will not make her the one. I name those because it is a couple of my favorites when I am cheating from trying to eat right every single day. Male or female, I wholeheartedly believe it is great to be career and business driven. You have goals. We should all have goals. You want to have an inheritance for your children's children. (Proverbs 13:22). That is a blessing. However, do not forget to check motives at the door. We must do a heart check with ourselves first. It is no secret many lavish things men buy is to attract a certain type of woman. In doing so, make sure that woman is godly (if that is your desire) and genuinely loves you for you. Is she willing to take the train with you instead of having a personal car pick her up? Can she take rideshare with you or do you have to pull up in a foreign vehicle? Let us not change who we are for love. Let us learn to be better version of ourselves now. Be the true you. Do the work. Once that person comes into your life attracted to the amazing energy you have as a whole being, the cooking will not matter. You can have a couple of dishes up your sleeve and be the best at ordering take out for every other meal. The person God has for you will love you. The hard working, inspiring 6 figures will be enough to stay around. You will not have to fine dine every night and continuously lavish for someone to stay with you. God's best will not require materialistic things.

Sometimes we can be the right key at the wrong door. If you have ever heard the saying, you will never be good enough for the wrong people, that is basically the same thing. God makes no mistakes. He prepares us for who he has for us. That does not mean we should not work to be better but work for yourself not for someone else. If you are at doors that do not open, thank God in the process. He is saving you for so much more. I truly look back at what I thought I wanted and cannot be more grateful for doors not opening. As the key, when the right door is in front of you, it will open, and your spirit will connect with everything on the inside.

We are all guilty of trying to force open a door based off the wrong things. I put too much time in this thing so I think I will stick it out. I have been posting so much on social media people already have a prospective about us so I will make this work. The skin, height, build, face, is everything. So, they may have a significant other, but they are not married yet, or they are married but not happily allegedly. I want this door. These are all wrong doors and wrong reasons for wanting to be at the door. Even if you can break in, your spirit will never connect with what is inside. You may be able to fake it on the surface, but is it even worth it when you know deep down it is not of God? That is rhetorical the answer should be no. God's door will not be forced open and it will not be shared with anyone else. It may even be a door that needs some gardening done. You may have passed by this very door numerous times simply because it was not groomed to your standard. I can promise you the door will be before you at the right time. Once inside you will have the instant spiritual connection. Please be mindful when I say spiritual it is more than getting butterflies, hot and bothered, or excited by the dollar bill y'all. When rooted in Christ, there will be no other way to explain it. You will be the perfect key for this door.

Calvin and I were in the same room so many times before we met. Had I met him any time before I did, he would not be my husband. Y'all, I was a mess! The patience Calvin has, I would have taken advantage of and considered him too nice. While I am still a storm at times, he did not deserve who I was at all before God revamped my mind and life. He truly has the best me. God had to prepare me for the calling that was on his life. God had to prepare me for the calling on my own life. I also know Calvin was being prepared for me. I am not easy to handle. I have a past. I have my personal issues that will send a weak man not rooted in Christ running. I know this because it has happened to me before. The time I met my Calvin I was completely single; I was not even texting anyone on that level. It was the same for him. I am not saying the way we met will be the same for you. We are all different and we date differently. I am saying it will work when it is God. Your key will be the right key for that door. You will know this was God ordained. You will be what God prepared your spouse for and vice versa. While you will continue to grow, hopefully since that is the goal, you will grow together. That means changing for the better. Not because that person wants you to change, but because you genuinely want to be better for yourself and for your ministry of marriage. I am the messenger and witness that God will make sure you can be vulnerable and unapologetically you with your significant other.

Ch. 22
Fad or Forever

I am a lover of food. I know I have mentioned it before, but it is so worth mentioning again. I love to eat. I love to cook. I love trying new cuisines and recipes to eat and cook. Making reservations for different restaurants, checking the menu online before going, and then seeing what is on the menu to make sure nothing else has popped up new between my reservation and arrival is my routine. I order one thing I know I would love and one thing I have never tried before which is appealing and exciting to me. I can taste a dish and know the ingredients used to reach this level of deliciousness. I even go home and reinvent the dish if it was worth the time and effort. Glossing over so many menus they usually change with what is popular at the time. It seems like there is always a dish, rather it be an appetizer, side dish, or even entrée that is a must have. Everyone adds it to their menu in one form or another.

Living in Nashville there are not many local restaurants or even many national chains that do not have some form of Nashville hot chicken. You can get it in a salad, you can get it on a stick, you can get it vegan, you can get it mild which tends to defeat the hot altogether, but you get what I am saying.

At one point, all the hip and popular restaurants were pushing Brussel sprouts. People were obsessed suddenly as if this was not a vegetable on the top ten list of most disgusting vegetables two years earlier. It was on the list of foods to avoid at all costs. I refuse to believe I am the only person who had Brussel sprouts on my ewww gross list. How it became such a popular food is unbeknownst to me. Maybe because of a magazine spread showing the rich and famous eating them or some food blogger with 1 million followers encouraged it for several reasons. Either way, there was a push like what I see quite often, and the demand was beyond crazy like every other time. Great for the farmers. They deserve the boost for sure. I saw them on so many menus I figured to be a functioning restaurant it was sort of an obligatory duty to add them. Roasted, sauteed, with bacon, with honey, with bacon and honey, the list was never ending. Once that fad slowly ended, another one came.

I believe every child has enjoyed a Lunchables. Even if your parent did not want you to have the preservatives in the prepared containers in the store, you would have some form of meat cheese and crackers or maybe simply cheese and crackers. Then comes the charcuterie boards. This is fancy and French and now extremely expensive on a menu as if this was not the light refreshments served at cocktail hour of any event in the past. I will give it to Memphis. At every local BBQ eatery, you can get a tray of sausages, cheese, crackers, and even peppers for a nominal fee. However, this wave of charcuterie boards is the new go to food that is taking over. I have seen numerous virtual classes to teach how to make them since with the global pandemic many places are not allowing large groups in restaurants. I think it is awesome to have those classes. I am sure there is a perfectly great French way to coordinate a charcuterie board. However, I also know soon this fad will go away. People will either be on to the next great thing or realize they are paying too much money for deli meat and cheeses.

This brings me to my thoughts of how thankful I am God does not go on to the next best thing. I am yours, and you are mine. (Isaiah 43:1 NIV). God is ours forever. He never stops loving us. He never stops caring for us. We do not deserve it. Period. At no point do I think God is so amazing because I deserve it. Absolutely not. I am simply thankful He is not obsessed with fads as we are. Yes, I am guilty as well. I think about all the trends I hold on to while they are cool then drop like a bad habit when it is no longer cool for the culture. When I was in middle school, I would rock the Saucony sneakers and my First Down oversized coat. We saw it in the music videos, so we wanted to wear them too. As soon as I got to high school that was no longer a thing, and I all but buried my coat in the deepest part of my closet never to be seen again. I refused to be caught in last season's fashion trends. It was time to switch it up right away. In was no different in college. My freshmen year was a determining year. As such, I wore my gaucho pants and button-down blouses with all the bright, colorful plastic jewelry my brown skin would allow. It was set off with a thick belt not much smaller than that of a WWE title champion title holder would carry on his shoulder in the ring. I look back at those pictures thinking wow. I cannot believe that was the style. It was, and for that juncture no one could not tell me and my friends we were not showstoppers. However, once it was no longer trendy to wear, we all look back at those pictures with slight disdain remembering the tremendous times we had while regretting some of those then trendy outfits.

Even more reason I am so thankful that God is God, and I am not. Jesus Christ is the same yesterday, today, and forever. (Hebrew 13:8). He is not changing up the menu to get costumers, no matter the level of loyalty that comes through the door. He does not push yesterday's styles to the side because they do not fit today's trends. His Word does not change and yet still is as relatable today as it was two thousand years ago.

Think about the people you became attracted to because of a feature they had that was such a turn on. When you got to know them or that feature was not a trending topic, did you still want to date that person? Think about it the other way around. It usually works both ways. When I was younger, I remember the super skinny girls with long, straight hair was the thing. That is what everyone wanted. Women were dying to get those thin model-like bodies. I knew I would never be skinny, but I wanted to be as small as possible so no one would call me fat. Today, that has completely changed. People are spending money on Brazilian Butt Lifts or BBLs to get the full figured curvaceous, shapely figure eight look. Since this is closer to my figure you would think I am the go-to. Yet it's not perfect because it's not bought so natural bodies are considered second rate by many stars, celebrities, and people who want to be like them. This too is a fad and will change once something else comes along.

This is not to make anyone feel bad about their personal decision. I wholeheartedly believe that if you are not happy with yourself, inside or outside, it is a personal decision to change for the better. I know some people think BBLs are a waste of money, for some it is a huge confidence boost that has nothing to do with being with a baller. One thing I pray is that whatever change you consider, you do it with you and God in mind. And if you are not a believer, do it for you after weighing the pros and cons.

Simply remember, no matter the fad or what is pop culture at the time, God loves you. God desires you. He is looking at your spirit man. (1 Samuel 16:7). Of course, God wants us to eat good, look good, live good as Kingdom beings, but all of that is relative to who and where you are. Some of my circumstances, simply having something to eat was good enough for me. I remember laughing with a friend about my excitement to go into the office because at least water, tea and coffee was free. I was on the struggle bus, but God was steering that thing and never left me. God's love is forever. As the fads change, but there is nothing more comforting than knowing God and His love will last forever.

Ch. 23
Crushing on You

When I think of a crush it takes me back to my middle school days when I liked the cutest boy in the class or the most popular guy in my neighborhood. It was always infatuation and never anything profound. Yet, it felt so real at the time. I grew up in a very urban part of Memphis, South Memphis to be exact. At the corner was Al's Tasty Burger in with the best burgers and chili cheese dogs this side of the Mississippi River. Standing in front of Al's, across the street, was the apartments I frequent. This is where my big sister and I were from the time we got out of school until it was time to go home to sleep. So much was always happening on the corner. We loved it. We loved the excitement of the arguing couples, the upset mother going off on her child, the smell of the food from the firehouse right next door, and more than anything the young guys who hung around with the nice fits and sneakers on. At that time, they paid us no attention. But I was crushing hard on one. He always rocked a nice pair of Nike Air Max or Air Jordan. He had on crisp, starched baggy jeans and an oversized Tommy Hilfiger shirt. I remember thinking he is so cool. Obviously, he was into all the high school girls his age and paid me, my sister, and our friends no mind. Not to mention whenever one of the girls would ask who I liked I always said no one. I did not want people to think I had a crush on anyone especially not the older boys who hung out on the corner.

Fast forward to over a decade later. I was living in Michigan and in my first year of law school. While on Facebook, I get a friend request from my childhood crush Spooner. He liked a few pictures and within hours he was in my direct messages seeing how my day was. I was thinking this guy from the hood really has matured. He

165

wrote in complete sentences, he was a natural conversationalist, he was well versed in current events as well as sports and pop culture. We exchanged numbers and would talk on the phone or text for hours. I learned that Spooner did not finish high school, he had never worked a real job, he was a hustler, and had a child. All the signs were there to end the conversation. I should have blocked him on my cell and all social media platforms. However, I was intrigued. Intrigued because although I grew up in the same hood as him, I was always sheltered from the lifestyle he lived. Intrigued because he was somewhat of an entrepreneur and apparently did exceptionally well financially for himself. Intrigued because he was the type of guy my father had warned me about since I "became a woman" as he would call it. Yet, it was the first time I was able to have fun with no expectations. I did not expect anything from this man. I could never take him home, I could never openly date him, I could never marry him. I could have fun with him, and he would happily finance all the fun. We decided to keep our fun on the low. Spooner would visit me. We would take trips. I never told my family about him. Only a few of my close friends were even privy of our encounters. I was still in love with my high school sweetheart Eli, but he was husband material my dad was ready to marry me off to at any given moment. While Eli said nothing could ever come between our love, he was so distant from me I was practically begging for time and attention. I wanted to have fun with my forbidden fruit, my crush Spooner.

The fun lasted for a few months. During that time, he was financing my life and was giving me more time that I had to spare for myself. I even slipped up on studying to stay up talking to him. I would fall asleep with my phone in my hand and my law book on the other side of the bed. On visits, Spooner would conveniently oversleep so he could not go to church with me, or he would attend but not be present. Here we go again. I even mentioned at times I felt further away from God due to his presence. He would not say much in response. Things sort of got, not fun. Eli was in his feelings about my time being split. While Spooner was visiting me in Michigan, he told me to call Eli at that time to inform him he should have his own fun because I was happy. While that was only partially true I did just that. I know I broke Eli in that very moment. I was so happy with the time and attention I was receiving from Spooner; I did not think to mend that fracture at the time. Sometimes when one person is giving so little or particularly nothing, a little bit more seems like everything. The devil knows exactly where to creep in, those weak spots already troublesome. Later, my daddy had suspicions. The streets were talking. Things were getting back to him. Once his worst fear came true, he cut me off. No random daily conversations, no supportive speeches, no voicemails just checking to see how I was while I was in class. I was devasted, crushed. That crushing was one I could not bear. I spoke with Spooner about it; his response was he would pay for whatever my daddy was no longer paying and that it was time for me to grow up anyway. I was livid. He did not understand. He never had the relationship with either parent that I had with my daddy. He did not understand how it felt to have the communication door closed on me. Forget the money, I needed my daddy. I had already been so many years without him in the physical. I had ruined things with Eli, I was not going to ruin this too. This great daddy daughter relationship is what I prayed for in elementary while making up jobs my daddy did while he was doing an 11-year prison sentence. I could not lose him. In the meantime, Spooner started traveling to Atlanta more. Our conversations got shorter. The money was still flowing, but I no longer had his time which is what intrigued me the most. After social media stalking, I learned he had a girlfriend.

We talked, she told me all the details. She said he told her I was his cousin. I laughed because that was clearly a joke. Cousin was quite amusing. But I wanted to cry because I got played by someone who was supposed to be nothing but fun. Once Spooner knew that I was aware of his relationship, he tried to explain he was only fun to me and he wanted more, and I refused to grow up. It was not about growth, but he could not see that. I wanted to show him that I was there for him and that I would not give up on him like all the other people in his life he mentioned to me. I felt that I could do that as a friend. I was starting to see that maybe he forced people away from him. The time had already stopped. After those conversations, the money stopped. We tried to attempt being cordial, but that did not work due to his many lies. Either way, I could not change what happened, but I could start mending. I instantly called my daddy and told him he was right about everything. He simply said, "Daddy loves you," as he hopped on a plane to somewhere with his friends. A father's love is everything.

My daddy was never an "I told you so" kind of person. He was overprotective for a reason. He wanted to see better in his children. I loved him for that. It reminded me of my Heavenly Father.

Our Heavenly Father is our protector. In Psalm 12:5 the Lord says I will protect them from those who malign them. God did just that. He had to crush me for me to come to senses about my crush. No discipline seems pleasant at the time, it is rather painful. Later, however, it produces a harvest of righteousness and peace for those who have been trained by it. (Hebrews 12:11 NIV). That feeling of everything falling apart was overwhelming and at times unbearable, but I knew I could lean on God to put it all back together. For that strictness, I am forever grateful. No matter how much fun we have in the world, He is always ready and willing to accept us back. God never leaves us nor forsakes us. (Deuteronomy 31:6). I am a witness that you can always trust God's Word. He was always there. The men in my life disconnected from me, but I connected to my true Source. No amount of time or finances can compare to the True Source, Jesus. It was me that was away from Him. But He waited for me to reach my arms back out to Him. His love for me never changed. Psalm 145:18 says God is near to all those who call on Him in truth. While Psalm 34:18 says the Lord is near to the brokenhearted and saves the crushed in spirit. There is no doubt in my mind the crushing saved me.

If sharing my personal stories of defeat can do anything, I hope it can help someone else who has endured or currently endured some form of crushing. I have some takeaways that I want to share.

1. The crushing led to my pain.
   I was beyond hurt. That means hurt was at 100 and I was at 200. The emotional pain was so bad I almost considered physical pain for numbness. I did not, but I was close to it. I had no escape and had to endure it for then.

2. The crushing led to my panic.
   I felt like I had nothing and was grasping for anything to come back to me. I had been so dependent on others; now how did I gain my happiness? I felt so out of control and lost. I wanted to crawl under a rock.

3. The crushing led to my preparedness.
   I knew how it felt to have it all stripped away in the matter of what felt like moments. It prepared me to go without, it prepared me to lean solely on Christ. It prepared me to be alone and be okay with that. Alone did not mean lonely. It prepared me for situations

that were completely out of my control. I am still a work in progress with this one, but I am better.

4. The crushing led to my peace.
   After all the chaos, I turned to God. I received that inner peace that no one around me could give me. I knew it came from God. My peace was not determined by time, money, or a being. I smiled knowing God did that. Amid future trials, I kept that peace, and it remains with me.

***

From that crushing I learned that God could never fail me. I was traumatized from feeling like I let go of my everything to hold on to nothing only to learn that was all part of God's plan. In turn, God taught me that He was it for me. Even without a father, a man, a friend, He would still be present. And He was. And it prepared me for not being with the whole man although we did establish a friendship much later. It also prepared me for the hardest thing I ever dealt with, losing my father, my earthly king. Still, that one is tough. I feel that horrible stomach pain yet again. But I know my Heavenly Father crushed me back then to make way for the slightest amount of strength I could muster up when it was time to say "see you later on the other side" to my daddy and I knew he was at peace just no longer in my presence. When you go through the crushing, it is for your present and your future, but it is also for others. My crushing will always be part of my growth and testimony. Learn from the pain and panic. Move forward prepared and with peace that surpasses all understanding. (Philippians 4:6).

Ch. 24
Silent but Not Silenced.

I love to talk. Calvin will tell you I talk to my friends and at least one of my family members every day and sometimes multiple times a day. I never want to take for granted having such loving and close relationships. I do my best to foster those when possible. For those who do not know me, I am very reserved. When I start to feel you out, and I am comfortable in your space, I enjoy a good conversation. I am not the loud friend. I am the laughing friend. Everything is funny to me. That is simply because I can find humor in almost every situation. I believe this trait to be a blessing in disguise. Laughter is good for the soul. With so much going on in the world, we need more laughter. I am also the passionate friend about topics that are important to me. The passion comes off as aggression at times. I know as a litigator I can debate with the best of them, but some people in my circle rather not debate. I know some people who want people to agree with them. That is fine. However, if I do not agree, you will know it. I laugh and smile about almost everything, but two of my passions happen to be two very controversial topics: God and politics. Also, since I am a litigator who has done criminal work in my past, I love to discuss social injustices and how it impacts us daily.

I have learned when and how to handle a lot of these discussions. I keep a calm tone. I am respectful when others speak. I am still working on my facial expressions, but I never said I mastered this thing. It is a work in progress. Still, there are times that something is said in a conversation that brings up part of me that I thought was healed. When I heard this conversation, I felt like I was having an outer body experience and realized I am so far from where I need to be. That feeling is okay. That feeling that strikes you once you realize you need help with something you thought you had conquered. Yet, I did not want to let those around me know that I was even struggling with this because it was a life altering event I encountered and opening that wound up to others would have people feeling sorry for me and possibly wanting me to ball up in a circle and disappear. Still, what was being said in this conversation left me baffled and silent. I know I am being very cryptic here. I will tell you now if you do not want to hear a detailed mental playback of the night I was sexually assaulted just head over to the next chapter. This one gets real and all derived from a normal conversation with the girls.

Have you ever felt like your input could sway someone from being their true selves? Let me break it down before you answer that. I never want my own experiences invalid someone else's feelings. I believe we feel a certain way because of our own experiences, vantage point, upbringing, and other things personal to us. For those reasons, your feelings are valid. Have you been part of a conversation that someone says something that hits you to the core, but you do not let them know because you do not want their mind to change simply because you had experienced what they are speaking on? At this moment I am sure you are pondering asking one or two things: 1) what in the world is she talking about? And 2) where is she going with this? I will explain.

I have a group of friends in Nashville I call my "work friends" although we are no longer all coworkers. The group is comprised of five attorneys and another beautiful spirit who happens to love attorneys. We vary in age by almost fifteen years. We are all Black women, but we have all different backgrounds, upbringings, and experiences. While four of the six are Memphians, each of us has completely different views, passions, and triggers. I love our discussions and how, even when we disagree, we can acknowledge it and move on to the next matter at hand.

One day during a group video chat toward the end of 2020. Think about the growth of the me to movement and cancel culture at that time. We were discussing what constituted rape in our eyes. One of my friends who is a great debater said that a woman cannot claim rape if she did not say stop. With us all having legal backgrounds we asked her to elaborate. She said there must be verbal communication of stop, no, don't or something of that nature to constitute an unwanted act of intercourse (rape) because we cannot think a man, especially a stranger, knows our body language enough to know we do not want the sexual act. She believed that the mens rea or the intent to commit rape somehow was absent if the woman did not verbally say no. Please, do not stop reading. The intent to have sex with someone against that person's will is not determined by stop, no, or don't vocalized by the woman. However, as legal minds, we knew the intent to have unwanted intercourse had to be proven. It is harder to prove he had that intent, but it is still possible when given the totality of the circumstances. It is a very gray area. There is no Black and white. I know this. I know everything must be taken into consideration. As such, this is why so many rape victims do not pursue the case and nothing more.

The reason I could not say more is because I felt so small in that very moment. I felt like a pea sitting at a large dining table with a large screen in front of me. I never once screamed. I did not shout out STOP. NO. DON'T. Could I possibly be the reason he did not stop? Was it my fault? Did I appear as if I wanted it? The devil will have you perturbed at yourself.

January 2014 I was raped by a man I went on two dates with. He was not my type from the beginning, but I was doing everything I could to move on from my ex-boyfriend, the whole man I have discussed way too much.

From The Crushing to The Crown

I figured if I spent time with other men, I would get my mind off him. The guy and I went to a Mexican restaurant. We had superb food, but I could tell from the conversation he was not it for me. He talked about himself entirely too much. He talked about a future with me and did not know me. He was physically not my type at all. Light brown skin, brown eyes, short curly hair, about 6'3" or maybe taller and 350-400 pounds. He had muscles, but not much definition. After dinner he took me home and asked if he could come in. I told him that was not a good idea, but we should hang again. He texted me when he made it home and continued texting all week throughout the day. He said it was something about me, and he wanted to see me again soon. He explained he had just moved and wanted to do some shopping for his place. He felt a woman's touch would be nice. I met him at his place that weekend. He went to Home Goods to find some nice things to make his new apartment feel like home. Everything I suggested he shot down. I soon realized he did not need a woman's opinion at all. I hate shopping and was ready to go. We went back to his place and talked as he put up all the bathroom décor he had purchased. He told me he had dreams of what I cannot remember, but I knew I was not going to be part of them.

We had a drink, and I was letting him know I wanted to leave. He suggested I stay and laid me on the bed. My mind left me, or I have tried to forget all those details. I remember so much weight on me that I thought I would suffocate. Or was I holding my breath? That is still a faint memory. I remember squirming as much as possible and trying to push him off me with all the strength left in my body to no avail. I never screamed. I never said a word. I laid back until he got off me. I quickly put on my clothes with tears rolling down my eyes, grabbed my purse, and left. All the texts and calls stopped immediately. I never heard from him again.

Back to me being a pea in my seat talking to my girls about what we considered rape to be in our opinion. Because I never wanted them to see me as a victim, I remained silent. Princess can argue with the best of them. And originally, I was ready to say many things. When I remembered I never uttered stop, no, don't almost seven years earlier, I had no words left for that debate.

Had I told my friend about my traumatic experience I am not sure what would have been the result. Maybe verbal communication as a requirement would have come off the table. Maybe she would have told me I should have said something then. I know others would have tried to comfort me and apologize and I was not up for any of that. Ask my therapist, I could never say I was a victim of anything. I refused to admit it.

From this entire situation, I learned that healing from trauma is a process. Take the necessary steps to heal and trust the process. From the start I isolated myself. I did not even talk to my male best friend whom I talked to every single day. I was at my lowest. But God. Jeremiah 30:17 NIV says, "But I will restore you to health and heal your wounds, declares the Lord." The restoration did not come over night. I prayed and cried and cried and prayed. I was angry at God, at myself. I was fearful this man gave me something I could not get rid of and even fearful he would come after me. I knew his business gave him access to weapons and discretion. I hated myself. But I leaned on God, eventually. I did not go directly to Him. He was not with me when I laid there what felt like forever. I finally came around. I knew my only way of surviving this tragedy was through something more powerful than me. I journaled. Pages wet with tears I did not stop. I went to therapy. I know not everyone in the Christian community believes in therapy. However, I know God placed my therapist in my life for a reason. She got me through the darkest times, and she helped me get to the root of many of my problems. You can go years without a trigger then out of nowhere, you feel like you will crumble. Do not get down on yourself if you are 5 or even 10 years out from something and it still hurts.

I also learned that silence does not mean I am ashamed. Because I did the healing, I had no shame. I admit I was triggered, but I am victorious because God restored me and made me whole. (Luke 17:19 KJV). I was not the cause of my trauma, but I learned to do my part in the healing. Isaiah 61:7 NLT says instead of shame and dishonor, you will enjoy a double share of honor. I went through what I encountered to come out giving God the glory. (Romans 8:28). All the honor belongs to God. Instead of hanging my head, I am telling my story in hopes of someone else healing. The day I went to turn in information related to my sexual assault, I saw another attorney I know. She listened as the clerk said this is not a sexual assault case this is rape. I said I understand and peeked over my sunglasses. She asked me to verify the name of the victim and my name. She realized I was the attorney and the victim. She instantly felt sorry for me. I hated that feeling knowing I was pitied. The other attorney never spoke on it, but she has remained nice to me also greeting me with a warm smile. I am not sure if she ever realized her not changing up on me helped me through some tough times. For that, I refuse to be embarrassed by what someone else did to me.

I learned that my traumas could help someone else out of their painful pit. Your pit does not have to mirror mine, in fact, I pray it does not. I do not wish that feeling on anyone. I do know that despondent and miserable feeling does not differ much. That horrific feeling will haunt you and even manifest in the physical if you do not give it to God and let Him handle it. I did not take control of my life and all my problems went away. I gave God my life, and I was given the tools to handle my problems. Psalm

9:10 ESV says that those who know Your name put their trust in You, for You, O Lord, have not forsaken those who seek you. He has never let me down. Just as God has gotten me through everything else, He got me through this. I will say He is getting me through this. Even today I was triggered by a movie. This time I felt empowered and thankful I did not let this traumatic experience alter God's plan for my life. I have remained faithful through the pain. It is painful writing out what happened to me knowing others will read it, hoping others will read it. The best way to get through the pain is to deal with it. This is how I am choosing to deal with that situation. Victory is mine even in the silence.

Fast and Pray Your Way Through It

I enjoy an alcoholic beverage or two. Sorry if that makes me a bad Christian to anyone. I answer to God. My university was dry but still a party school, and I took full advantage. My girls and I would pregame which is basically drinking before you go drink with others. Once we got to our destination, we would drink more. I realize I would make myself a drink to sit and watch a movie in my dorm room. I remember sitting in front of my bed with my green cup filled with vodka and Hawaiian punch crying while Will Smith pursued happiness with his son. Princess, why do you desire to drink? It was a question I asked myself, but because I knew I was not addicted I did not think much more into it. I know everyone says they can stop when they want. It is so typical right. That was the story for law school as well. Drinking with friends after a major exam or during a study break was a release. Then I would have a drink while I studied. It was no big deal; I was on the dean's list after all. I remember when going home during law school break my daddy and I would ride around talking about everything and nothing. He would have his Newport lit cracking my window only a little, so I do not lecture him about the health-related issues of tobacco for the smoker and those around him. We would listen to some old school classics like David Ruffin and Womack and Womack. We would also bob our head to some dope beats while Jeezy or Styles P rapped. If it were a Sunday, we would almost certainly stop by the bootlegger. At this time, in Tennessee, you could not buy alcohol on a Sunday. Since we were going to South Memphis anyway, we would make a much-needed frolic. Daddy would only let me get wine, but I was fine with that. He would get Hennessey. That Sunday night, I would sip my wine and smile about the good times with Daddy that day. I was drinking alone again. While studying for the bar, Daddy called to have a serious conversation. My daddy felt I had a drinking problem. The conversation was not deep. It was basically him saying, "Princeeeessss! I gave up alcohol. I realize I am not setting the best example and the reason you have a problem is because you see me drinking all the time." I said, "Daddy I do not have a problem, but I think it's awesome what you are doing." I knew then I had to stop too. And I did. I remember telling Daddy around mid-March that I had not drank since the end of January. He was extremely proud. I did not drink for three months. If I am being honest, I did not realize it had been so long. Between my study schedule, the gym, and working two jobs, I did not have time to drink anyway.

The closer I got to God, I learned the importance of sacrifice and that leaning on substances is not the answer. I knew that fasting was spiritual and was done for reasons between that person and God. While I had partook in lent numerous times, I was never led to fast from alcohol. God put on my spirit to begin such. It was at random times for random periods of time, 30 days here, 21 days there. I was so full of the spirit I did not miss alcohol at all. My pockets surely did not miss it, because going out for drinks can be expensive. I enjoyed that time with my Heavenly Father. I drew closer to Him. He fed me on a level that cannot be explained. During my times of sobriety, God came to me in many ways. He informed me of things I could never have been prepared for otherwise. The more I fasted the closer I felt to God. I begin doing this with social media as well. It took up so much of my time, I knew that I could be much more productive if I was not strolling down my timeline. And I was. I can remember an old friend telling me I take so many breaks from social media I should simply get off the apps altogether. I laughed. People will not always understand why you do the things you do. That is because they are not meant to understand. Please never felt any type of way about that because God spoke to you about what He desires from you. The sacrifices you make are not required for others and never try to make it such.

I do thank God for the friends who joined me in the fasts and the sacrifices. We did not always fast from the same things. We did not all pray for the same thing. But I always asked that we pray for God's best. It was especially important that our desires aligned with His for me. That remains the same. In the end of 2017, the Lord told me to fast from alcohol. I was like here we go again. Time to prepare for something epic. I say this because through fasting and prayer God prepared me for the biggest tragedies in my life. After being fired and jobless right before I got my bar results the second time around, I trusted God enough to follow through with a move into a new apartment with a new roommate. I know had I not been rooted in Christ when my father was murdered, I would have been committed to a psychiatric ward. So, when God told me to fast, I was ready with caution because I was not sure what was coming. A couple of my friends agreed to join in. We would do so for 60 days. We were all ready for the clarity it would bring. In prayer and communing with God, He told me 365 days instead of the original 60. And he also told me this was only for me so do not attempt to persuade anyone else to join me. When I tell you God knows us so well! I was ready to jump in that group text and say God said WE need to fast for a year. He stopped me before I could start. I informed the others the fast had been extended for me and I would be doing a year.

In this time God did miraculous things. He warned me of temptations to come. I meditated on scriptures. I knew I would be attacked and wanted to be ready. A guy entered my life that February. He was a counterfeit. He did not last long. People from my past started jumping in my DMs and texts. My block game was strong. I was not sure what God was doing. I knew that temptation did not come from God. But I also knew I had tests to pass. Yet, did God forget I had already told Him I was done kissing frogs. I had been waiting on God's best for years at this point. While it was extremely easy for me to detect those from outside my life coming in, I did not realize I was being infiltrated from the inside. That was a prayer like no other. When someone you deem a friend is physically attracted and emotionally connected to you and you to him, you must be careful. The Lord worked on me and on us. Once we knew the friendship could no longer be, we had to part ways. Even when I wanted to stay friends, God removed him out my life because the friendship was done. That season was over. I was later grateful.

During this time, I was introduced to the now love of my life. It was a normal Thursday originally. After work, I went to the gym. I showered at the gym then rushed out to get on I-40E headed to Mount Juliet, a small family-oriented town outside of Nashville. I knew I was headed to meet a guy my mentee's dad said would be a good match for me. Our first date was the first time we met. I was not nervous. I did a little research prior to this meetup, so I knew his profession and that he was attractive. We talked for hours. It took almost an hour for us to place our order because the food was not as important in the moment. If you know either of us, you know food is life for us, so this was a sign something miraculous was happening. After the initial meeting, I knew I wanted to see him again. We planned to meet again that Saturday for tennis. He was late calling me for tennis. I started freaking out. So much crossed my mind, but for some reason I felt he would not ghost me although I only knew him for two days. He finally called and was very apologetic. His praise team rehearsal had run over because the Holy Spirit was flowing. I was in awe. We met up to play tennis. I should mention here that tennis is hard and not my strong suit at all. He taught me a lot. He was patient with my lack of athleticism. We talked about so much more, and yet it still felt like it was not enough time. We were both traveling soon but promised to keep in touch. We did just that. We continued to text and talk every day from that day forward. He became my best friend and I affectionately referred to him as My Cowboy. His mama named him Calvin, so he is Calvin to the rest of the world. Being that Calvin grew up in the country, loved country music, and could be seen frequently in cowboy boots and a hat, it was fitting.

God brought me His best during one of the biggest fasts in my life. Had I not been in the Spirit, I could have thought of numerous reasons why it would not work. We were so different. We came from different upbringings, we lived our lives differently, and we liked different college football teams. The sports thing may not be big for some, but that was one of the biggest hurdles for me. Could I live happily with an Alabama fan? I kept having to tell myself at least it is the SEC, and we are in the same conference. Deep down I am also thinking how we even deal on gamedays. Calvin's birthday is five days after mine. I am a huge birthday person. I celebrate my entire month, then throughout the zodiac time span. Five days after my birthday, I am usually still celebrating my day for another two or so weeks. His birthday ruins all of that. It was a lot to consider. All jokes aside, Calvin loved me for me. My passion for politics and the law he embraced immediately. I was glad to know he was intrigued by what I did and wanted to learn more. Because God had prepared me for him, he got the best version of me. I believe it was the same vice versa. Calvin informed me he too prayed and fasted for me. We both were waiting to be sexually active until marriage. However, he had been waiting his entire life. God had told me the man He had for me would not hesitate at my celibacy, but I had no idea he would still be a virgin. My Cowboy, my Calvin had a list! I said a guy with a list wow. He said everyone advised him to let the list go, but he felt God would deliver. He also said I was everything on that list and things he did not know he needed as well. God showed out as He always does.

When the clock struck 12:00am January 1, 2019, I had my first drink with Calvin and friends. We had a great time, and I was thanking God for no confusion, no blinders, no outside voices. It was me and God in this thing. Several days later, God called me into another fast. Every January it was customary to do a corporate fast with my church. This was to start the year of trusting and leaning on God. I did not blink. I was ready to see what God had in store. While in this fast with my church, I was still all in and ready to see what God desired of me and for me. Calvin proposed. We had only known each other seven months and had been officially courting for six months. It is not about our own timelines. God has the perfect timing. I also got promoted on my job during this fast. God said it was time for elevation. I was beyond blessed. I had so much peace about the things that God had placed in my life. Did I mention I failed tests during my fast? I was not perfect by far. But I thank God I serve a perfect God.

I learned that fasting and prayer was not simply about preparing for the tragedies in my life, it was also about preparing for the good. God wanted me to lean entirely on Him and not the world or culture at times when outside voices are at their loudest. I had so many people in my ear, but I was able to tune them all out because God's voice was so distinct. For you, the fast could be from secular music, certain foods, certain activities. There is no textbook answer or universal timeframe. God has specific strategic plans for us all. His Word is clear in that it can take fasting and prayer to cast out certain demons. (Mark

9:29). It is the same with the demons in our own lives. Allow God to declutter your mind. Temporarily remove anything that is considered a true sacrifice in your life. Pray and set specific time aside to be with God alone. He will do the rest.

With every decision, I do my best to take it to God first. I pray and commune with God not just when things get hard, but because He is a friend and deserves time like every other relationship in your life. Whenever I am making a major decision, I fast and pray. Since married, Calvin and I fast and pray together. Mathew 6:16-18 reminds us that our fasting should not be known to others, but that it is something between you and God. Therefore, this is not something we broadcast to the masses, but we do reach out to other prayer warriors to pray for us or with us when led to do so. We do it to receive necessary guidance and answers from Christ; we do it to grow spiritually; and we do it to ensure that we never lose sight that God is in control, not our flesh. The result is not always what we want. This enables us to lean on the Spirit and not person, a substance, or a place holder. At no point have I made Calvin my god. He is not. He is the man I love with all my being, but the love I have for him will never come before God. I know it to be true with him as well. In fact, this love draws me closer to God. I am no longer in an unhealthy relationship thinking my happiness depends on someone else. God completed me before I knew my husband existed. I found my joy and happiness before Calvin found me. I refuse to result back to the toxic thinking that someone else completes me or that man can cause my happiness. I confer with Calvin about everything, but my joy and happiness come from above. The reason I love him so is that his love for me is second to Christ just how it should be.

Whatever you are believing God for or needing advice on, prayer alone may not get you there. Fast and pray.

Wait on God to deliver even if it is not what you desire. Rejoice while waiting. He prepared you and loved you enough to spend the time to carve out His best job, home, spouse, friend circle, mentor, therapist, doctor, coping mechanism, passion to name a few. Love Him enough to listen and yield to His Word. Love God enough to fast and pray in faith that it is already done.